NAMING
BECKETT'S
UNNAMABLE

NAMING
BECKETT'S
UNNAMABLE

Gary Adelman

Lewisburg
Bucknell University Press
London: Associated University Presses

Associated University Presses
2010 Eastpark Boulevard
Cranbury, NJ 08512

The paper used in this publication meets the requirements of the American National Standard for Permanence of Paper for Printed Library Materials Z39.48-1984.

Library of Congress Cataloging-in-Publication Data

Adelman, Gary.
    Naming Beckett's unnamable / Gary Adelman.
        p. cm.
Includes bibliographical references and index.
    ISBN 0-8387-5573-9 (alk. paper)
1. Beckett, Samuel, 1906—Prose. I. Title.

PQ2603.E378Z52 2004
848'.91409—dc21

                                                    2003012184

To Phyllis

and the memory of my parents

Contents

Acknowledgments

I would like to thank Elaine Fowler Palencia for the weekly sessions that extend back two books before this one, at which we would discuss and try to sharpen the work of writing as I turned it out. Thanks, Elaine, for your skill as an editor, constancy, and friendship.

My close friend, a retired entomologist, Stanley Friedman, took up the challenge of reading *How It Is* aloud. I am obligated to him for my deep infatuation with that novel, and to a late friend, also a scientist, Arthur Ghent, who enjoyed discussing Beckett's beetles biting-and-being-bitten view of human nature in *How It Is*, and who contributed to my understanding of the novel.

Graeme Malcolm, professional narrator and actor, literally electrified me with his reading of the trilogy. Hearing Malcolm perform the voice of the Unnamable was the starting point of this book.

I am indebted to two graduate students, Elizabeth Savage and Heather Zadra, who worked with me and for me in several capacities, and especially in helping me advance the progress of this book in manuscript.

I am very sorry that my late father will never see this. So much about life was "delicious" to him. High on that list was the daily routine with my mother; and just about as high were the opportunities to advise and comfort his kids. He would have been beaming with pride as he leafed through a copy of this book.

If only I could find the spell of words to convey you, mother, your wonderful youthfulness, and the feeling of you present now in all things. It was your spirit and temperament I inherited, and so my love for Beckett—his irreverence and dark hilarity, the fierce dirges and rollicking horseplay, the strange hope, and the "intimate" story of the "life said to have been mine above in the light before I fell."

It's pretty certain that this book would have been a manuscript in a drawer if I were not the lucky guy to whom Phyllis, my wife, gave her heart, mind, confiding eye, and even a kidney. Thanks, Phyllis, for taking charge of the last part of the manuscript process, double-checking everything, from the submitted manuscript, through the galleys, to compiling the index.

I also wish to thank the editors of the journals in which printed parts of this book first appeared: Susan Firestone Hahn of *TriQuarterly*, Morton Levitt of *Journal of Modern Literature*, and Mark Rudman of *Pequod*. Thanks, Mort, for going out of your way for me with advice. And thanks are due also to my friend and colleague, Herbert Marder, who gave me a written critique on a part of this work.

Introduction

This book concerns Samuel Beckett's major prose, 1946–1970. *The Unnamable* is the soul of the book, the way it keeps recurring in my thinking about Beckett's prose. Kafka is hardly less central as a touchstone, an illuminating point of reference. Central also is an independence I have felt from certain establishment precepts about Beckett, chiefly, that you misread him if you foreground story; that you misconstrue him by imagining a center of coherence; that your primary function as a critic is to note and explicate his philosophical concerns and to show the workmanship, the evolution of his aesthetics, and his writer's tricks. There is a protocol attached to all of this canonized by Ruby Cohn (2001) and long practiced by the most established of Beckett's critics, James Knowlson and John Pilling (1980), for example; chiefly, to limit yourself to pointing out what is precisely there; to hint at how it holds together; to show where a work fits in relation to another; to show similarities, adumbrations, and developments between one work and another; and to avoid interpretations as well as arguments with other critics.

A quick look at *Enough* illustrates what I mean by my independence. *Enough* is one of those short, cryptic pieces Beckett wrote in the 1960s. It has a first-person protagonist-narrator—a voice telling its story. I think it is the voice of a mad old lady unhinged by an experience that befell her in her maidenhood. Here is her voice:

11

I did all he desired. I desired it too. For him. Whenever he desired something so did I. . . . When he told me to lick his penis I hastened to do so. I drew satisfaction from it. We must have had the same satisfactions. . . . One day he told me to leave him. . . . Gone from reach of his voice I was gone from his life. . . . He must have been on his last legs. . . . I cannot have been more than six when he took me by the hand. Barely emerging from childhood. . . . All I know comes from him. . . . Though very bowed already he looked a giant to me. In the end his trunk ran parallel with the ground. . . . If the question were put to me suitably framed I would say yes indeed the end of this long outing was my life. . . . Bent double heads touching silent hand in hand. While all about us fast on one another the minutes flew. . . . It is then I shall have lived then or never. . . . If I had looked back I would have seen him in the place where I had left him. . . . In the years that followed I did not exclude the possibility of finding him again. . . . Or of hearing him call me. . . . But I did not count on it unduly. For I hardly raised my eyes from the flowers. And his voice was spent. . . . I can feel him at night pressed against me with all his twisted length. . . . With his upper hand he held and touched me where he wished. Up to a certain point. The other was twined in my hair. . . . We lived on flowers. So much for sustenance. . . . Now I'll wipe out everything but the flowers. No more rain. No more mounds. Nothing but the two of us dragging through the flowers. Enough my old breasts feel his old hand.[1]

Cohn says of this "achronological tale"[2]—that builds accretively on the four different accounts of the couple's separation, and out of postures, landscapes and other repetitive details— that it "traces a timeless liaison nourished by the flowers of rhetoric,"[3] and that "Strikingly, the couple is at once human and mythic, a voice and a pen, experience and its narration, a text-in-progress and its own fictionality."[4] Knowlson and Pilling think that *Enough* explores what happens when Beckett "banishes personality (in the accepted sense)" from his story, banishing, that is, "the dishonesty and spuriousness of [a narrator] substantializing himself in the text under the mask of 'I.'" They think of the story as an allegorical work on "the relationship between different aspects of the self which has been Beckett's main area of interest for many years."[5] "The narrator has failed to retrieve the older self and can only retrieve him at all through the medium of imagination." The memory becomes a fiction "offer[ing] the only 'calmative' that is worth anything."[6]

All this may be true. But there is a persistent impression about the story that has been ignored by the critics: it is nasty. Beckett can be seen to be writing riddles[7] in his later work. This one remains vaguely impenetrable to me. Only, I feel the impact of its smarminess. The speaker is mad, that Blakean madness of preserved virginity, of ten thousand days and nights guarded by fiery cherubs. *Enough* is Thel telling her story, still a virgin after that one terrible experience.[8] Thel speaks to worms and flowers, earth's humble creatures, until shocked by horror of horrors, stench of open earth, passion and death—adult life, in short— she flees back to her vales of Har, crimson sanctuary of onanistic adolescence. The old fellow may be the self that never developed, the adult experience from which she, epicene, androgynous, shrank. A mad old lady's remembrance of terror, when blood shook her heart, everything filtered out but the trickle of a connection that haunts her as the one momentous occasion of her life. Enough that she has that, an old, old man bowed to the earth, who touched her and whose penis she licked, and whom she left after walking round and round the earth through bowers of flowers. Or, enough, we cannot listen any longer to the childlike voice in the old lady's body, the chirrupy-sweet, demented voice of shocked and starved desire. It is just this that many critics leave out: the story. Beckett is a writer of stories.

How sad it would be if Beckett's prose (with the exception perhaps of *Murphy* and *Watt*) was not being read because of being perceived as the specialty of "professor types." Martin Amis inveighs against Beckett (in a recent memoir, *Experience*), performing over dinner with Rushdie an imitation of characteristic Beckett prose. "All you need is maximum ugliness and a lot of negatives. 'Nor it the nothing never is.' 'Neither nowhere the nothing is not.'"[9] This senseless, repetitive jabber, or "quaqua," is Amis's idea of Beckett. I know his problem: he confuses Beckett's prose with the academic praxis meant to illuminate it. Moreover, his distrust and distaste of what he takes to be Beckettian he gets from his novelist father and Philip Larkin, who intensely disliked writing that they felt was too complicated. I wish I was wrong, but I don't think writers, any more than the general reader, have found Beckett's prose. If they discovered the saga embedded in *The Unnamable*, that would be another matter (though they can't be put on to it by Beckett's commentators, who don't discuss it).

The Unnamable is the story of a hero fighting for some remnant of self, an "I," struggling not to be incorporated while breathing the air of the corporate, immersed in the language of the corporate. Belonging means perishing, means abdicating identity. Somehow the hero has to keep caring about something that so easily slips away; everything about human existence ministers to its slipping away—that is, the "I," the sacred self.

The very essence of being human, thought, becomes an enemy. Thinking is dangerous. Thought tends to be palliative. The effort to understand his situation, conceptualize, portray, take control, place himself above himself, call the shots, minimize the fear, dull the pain, stereotype his struggle—it's treacherous. It is hard not to let go and sink into the anonymity of human existence. The "I" can do nothing but hold out against the forces arraigned against it. No love, no being knitted into community, no bonds, no gainful employment, no doormat for dirty feet. Struggling on is a matter of conditioning; it's got to become a reflex—the mind in relentless high gear, racing, paranoid, vigilant, obsessive, the individual always fugitive.

It's no life. He has no defenses. He has no hopes. All he can do is try to go on, and on. I find him enthralling, much more so than the glamorous Prometheus of Shelley's vision. Truth need not be an issue to the reader, though the hero's mind may be very similar to that of a schizophrenic. Paranoia is a survival skill to a mind alert to the sacredness of self and the manifold threats to its existence. His "I," like a precious, fragile flame, exists only so long as he can keep elaborating on the saga of his persecutions.

Be agog, poets, it is the epic poem of our time—how the Unnamable perseveres in his struggle not to disappear, to "smother in a throng."[10] To be he must think, but there are three distinct dangers to thinking. First, he must not doubt that it is he who is thinking. He must own his thoughts, credit them to himself. He cannot stop thinking altogether; that's to go under. In extremis, danger number one is to concede that he can't make out whose voice it is and so slip away dispossessed, or, as it is in the conceit of the novel, into human existence. The second danger (already briefly noted) is that he will use thought for any one and all of the positive reinforcements fictionalizing his situation affords, including respite, momentary escape from the feeling of continuously being at bay. The return to himself from such relaxation is perilously depressing. Telling stories only weakens him, for a big motive underlying the need is self-pity—the reaching out for companionship, understanding, consolation. In every way storytelling is a corruption of his will, a doing commerce, a trafficking within the incorporating maw of existence.

No, nix to the powerful need to be soothed. That's why the heroes of the Unnamable's canonical fictions, Molloy and Malone, are deadbeat loners.

The third danger is to plan ahead, engineer a strategy, regularize his moves. Words, paradoxically, are his only camouflage, his wings, his element, the amazing spittle of words his unmistakable signature, yet in using them he risks becoming a social creature, one of millions. There can be no capitulation to a system; to catch sight of himself mechanized must destroy his will to go on. When, in fact, he comes to see himself as maneuvers, tactics, branchings and interbranchings of thought, his very being nothing but a grid, a repetitive pattern, his end nearly comes: like a crazed beast prowling in a cage, he becomes frenzied; going on becomes torture.

No systems, no fortifications. Being for him is a saga of indefatigable defensive moves, a constant talking to himself, a rousing of energy, a keeping before him the ongoing history of his persecutions. That's the crux of it, being clear about what's at issue and about his vulnerabilities.

Telling stories sustains him while being his greatest weakness. Writing is the genesis of a slow extinguishing of the imagination. He cannot survive sitting tight in a corner weaving like a spider. He must be on his toes, dancing, so to say, on the edge. No hideaway corners, no fortifications. His strength to go on lies in his being vulnerable.

After the romantic poets and the modernists, Beckett took the next giant step toward validating the sacredness of the self, operating in a world wherein existence had become inimical to the sacred.

The remarkable story embedded in *The Unnamable* may as well be the secret password of an inner sanctum of Beckettians, who guard it from the reading public like Masons.

All of Beckett's major ideas are found either in *The Unnamable* or can be illuminated by that text. *Texts for Nothing*, in some ways a coda to the trilogy, has the writer-hero playing taps at his own funeral. Post-trilogy, Beckett's oeuvre illuminates what can only be called a key, revivifying discovery: the lust to torture and desire to escape pain define the species. The self wishes to be engaged with another self in the interest of pain. As perceived in *How It Is*, it is all a matter of stinging and being stung, human existence likened to an endless track of countless beetles, each biting the one ahead and being bitten from behind. In light of this discovery, notions of transcendence and of indwellingness of spirit, and their types and symbols, are occasions for the writer-witness to play. When the narrator-protagonist of *How It Is* thinks of praying, the idea amuses him: "seen from behind on my knees arse bare on the summit of a muckheap."[11] He feels inspired, offers God his rectum, and breaks forth in ribald, snarling mockery, like Dante's Vanni Fucci, who "raised his hands/with both the figs, crying: 'Take them, God, I'm/aiming at you!'"[12] Obliging the species to show its face revivifies Beckett. We live in a world of matter and pain, all *Inferno*, or, rather, more specific to Beckett, the world of the concentration camp.

The metaphor of the writer as a condemned Jew is powerfully evoked in *The Unnamable* and implicit everywhere. Details of Beckett's living hell in the trilogy are clearly drawn from Hitler's camps. *Texts for Nothing* is improvisations on the writer's hell, and though ostensibly having little to do with concentration camps, that world represents life in the writer's ambivalence between world and imagination. *Texts* might be subtitled "to Kafka, with love," for Kafka like Beckett felt the "forsake all hope" of either choice. In *How It Is*, the metaphor of the writer as Jew has clearly changed from that of victim to torturer and victim. In the transformative vision of the last part of that novel, the spur to creativity is torture, *a* to *b*, *b* to *c*, *c* to *d*, in an infinitely expandable line of torturers and victims.

I confess to repeatedly striving to get the Unnamable in my clutches—of trying and failing to draw a grid of his interconnecting thoughts, I mean the every-which-way of his relentless dodging, the linkages that are the channels through which he flashes. Or would such a grid be little more than an X-ray of him?—the soul gone, no tracer sparks of motion, no voice, and hence really nothing. Even so, it's been a sore temptation to try. Must I have his soul in my clutches? I think I must if it is criticism I write. Beckett goes much further—in our clutches if we would be quickened. Possessing the soul of another, control, sadistic violation, becomes the primal law of creation in his take on the world after the trilogy. In the beginning was the lust for torture. The prospect rouses the imagination from inanition. It is "how it is" in the world of the novel by that name.

My persistent desire to have the Unnamable replicated as a grid, caged, mine for the demonstration, brings to mind a subtle remark by the narrator of *The Lost Ones*. "Such harmony only he can relish whose long experience and detailed knowledge of the niches are such as to permit a perfect mental image of the entire system."[13] *Harmony* is the perfect word because the relishing of the torture is aesthetic. However, capturing the Unnamable is impossible. He cannot be made a demonstration because he resists capture so successfully. Still, here's the book, a fabric of invention, and there is you, unwary reader, a situation allying me with the narrator of *Imagination Dead Imagine* and the officer of Kafka's "In the Penal Colony." Won't you take a seat?

NAMING
BECKETT'S
UNNAMABLE

1
The *Nouvelles*:
Preparing for the trilogy

Beckett wrote four stories in French in 1946 using anonymous, first-person protagonist-narrators: *First Love, The Expelled, The Calmative*, and *The End*. Numerous intertextual references link the stories, which can be seen as stories told by the narrator of *The Calmative*. There are two main themes. Three of the stories are about a person at a loss as to how to go about living, a person adrift, repeatedly being expelled from refuges, shelters, every eviction a repetition of having been kicked out of the family house, and, initially, of having been born. The three narrator-protagonists are alike enough to be taken as the same person, a persona of the narrator of the fourth story telling stories about himself, two of them when young and not yet hopeless, and one when old and hopeless. The second theme is a portrayal of the writer's vision of himself in relation to the nightmare of life, and his inexplicable going on with his storytelling despite its failure to alleviate despair. The four stories opened the way for Beckett to the trilogy.

The stories are Beckett's first in French and were written in an order different from that which appears in *The Complete Short Prose*. Ruby Cohn (2001) dislikes the ordering of the *Nouvelles* according to an interior chronology, for this arrangement implies plot development and closure. It "obscures the calculated indeterminacy of the stories." *The End*, she notes, was a "breakthrough story into plotless narrative."[1] Furthermore, "imposition of linearity would render most of the story digressive, and it is in these seeming digressions that Beckett magnetizes the attentive reader."[2] She points out that "the stories lack exposition, climax, or resolution," that they are "alogical," and that Beckett was on a course to pulverize what he believed to be "the arbitrary nature of narration"[3] by the elimination of paragraphs, the paring down of punctuation to commas and an occasional period, the dissolving of syntax itself, the spotlighting of a text as a self-conscious production, story become an adventure in and with language: language as speaking in vain, subject and object becoming indefinite, story as quest for how it is possible to say "I." "The combination of a first-person protagonist-narrator and the French language served as a liberating elixir for Beckett," Cohn says.[4] Critical engagement with the stories as stories is a personal affair that she leaves for the reader's contemplation.

Offering another view, J. E. Dearlove (1982) places the stories in the genesis of a developing aesthetic that foregrounds pattern. She says the four stories "blend into . . . diverse versions of the same basic story."[5] In her summary, "a figure, forced from an asylum, wanders about in search of some undefined thing; he meets someone who offers him an affectional relationship, but he rejects that offer and continues his search, ending alone."[6] Dearlove points out that the four characters are indistinct from one another. They lack names, work, shelter, background. They become interchangeable; their settings are interchangeable. The figures find nothing worthy of contemplation. Nothing is explainable. Companionship, friendship, generosity are refused, memory is banished. The figures exist without plans, without futures, without a sense of time. Beckett's aim, Dearlove says, is to reduce the characters to an archetypal existence. "Not even the fragile bonds of feeling are left to save man from his solipsism."[7] In this stripping away, Dearlove sees "the story of us all."

> Man is expelled into life where he makes a quest for a hypothetical grail which he never finds and may not believe in. During that journey he meets others who offer him order and relationships he ultimately rejects, ending alone—an isolated figure moving uncomprehendingly through his own version of the wasteland.[8]

I would ask the reader to note the aptness of this description for Kafka's *The Castle*. Later, in a final chapter, I describe *The Castle*'s importance to the genesis of the trilogy.

In my discussion of the stories, I place *The Calmative* after *The End* rather than before it, as it is in *The Complete Short Prose*, because it makes more sense to link the three that are stories told by the narrator of the fourth. By sketching the four stories, which are difficult to distinguish in retrospect because of repetition and lack of plot, we can discern the stance, characters, and concerns that come to maturity in the trilogy.

The surly, facetious narrator of *First Love* would like to shaft the "you" he addresses with a long middle finger. He speaks to his readers as to his shrink, promising to tell us all about his pains, "my strange pains, in detail."[9]

The narrator begins with a long side step to the memory of Lulu. He starts in riddles, though the answers become clear by the end when his tone has become confessional and we understand that the memory of Lulu haunts him. "I associate, rightly or wrongly, my marriage with the death of my father, in time" (25). He had loved his father. He frequently visits his father's grave. He infinitely prefers the smell of graveyards to the stink of the living, "their feet, teeth, armpits, arses, sticky foreskins and frustrated ovules" (26). I then to my graveyards and you keep to your public parks and beauty spots. Graveyards have become his theme. The pain of memories associated with Lulu and the death of his father brought him there. Moreover, he enjoys catering to our prurience.

He was evicted from the family house after his father's death quite promptly, with a small bequest, despite his pleading. His family packed him up while he was sitting in the outhouse. (Or did the irreverent charwoman with the bobbing ostrich feather hat in Kafka's "The Metamorphosis" sweep him off the premises? "Oh, . . . you don't need to bother about how to get rid of the thing next door. It's been seen to already.")[10] After he's gone, the family tuck themselves in their rooms. "[T]he blessed relief" and "come let's eat, the fumigation can wait" (29). Ah, people. "All those lips that had kissed me . . . those hands that had played with mine and those minds that had almost made their own of me!" (29). A sigh for Papa, who liked his presence in the house.

Lulu, he cannot remember her family name, he met by the bank of the canal on a bench backed by a mound of garbage and flanked by two dead trees. "What mattered to me in my dispeo-pled kingdom," he explains, was fog—not thinking, or feeling, as indifferent to "the disposition of my carcass" (31) as to my soul and the world. But, being twenty-five, prone on occasion to an erection, an attachment of sorts started.

He says that after a time he told her that he had had enough. "She disturbed me exceedingly, even absent. Indeed she still dis-turbs me" (32). It is the word *disturb*, popping out inadvertently, that carries him too suddenly ahead of his story, which brings forth a reflex of denial and anger:

> "And it matters nothing to me now, to be disturbed . . . and what would I do with myself if I wasn't? . . . not to mention not long now, not long till curtain down, on disturbers and disturbed, no more tattle about that, all that, her and the others, the shitball and heaven's high halls" (32).

This and more of the same having freshened the air and calmed him, he says that he "abandoned the bench . . . now that the air was beginning to strike chill, and for other reasons better not wasted on cunts like you, and took refuge in a deserted cowshed marked on one of my forays" (33). *Cunt* is British slang for the male of the species, though the narrator is inclusive. There, on a bed of cow dung, he found himself "tracing her name in old cow-shit. . . . And with my devil's finger into the bargain, which I then sucked" (34).

A note here on intertextuality among the four stories would merely point out how considerable it is. The same events, eccen-tricities, mannerisms, details, that is, taking refuge in a cow-shed, tasting shit, tend to merge the characters into one per-sona, and the stories into the telling of one narrator. These rhymes extend to blarney; but nothing can repel our prurience.

One day he returns to the bench. Her muff brings tears to his eyes. He asks her to sing a song. The game he plays, retreating from the bench until he can no longer hear her singing, then back and forth in and out of her sound, then out and breaking away, might be called doing it without doing it.

He returns to the bench some weeks later. Eventually she shows up and says she has a room. She has two rooms separated by a kitchen with running water and gas at the top of an old house. Flourishing his eccentricities, he describes his horror of her parlor—"Such density of furniture defeats imagination" (39)—which he consents to inhabit on the proviso that all the furniture be removed with the exception of a sofa (it is all stacked in a hallway between the room and the door out) and that she doesn't tax him much with conversation. The groans and giggles of her callers disturb him. He has learned from experience, he says, that clearing up one's feelings by asking questions is like trying to solve the riddle of God's existence by inquiry. "So a fat lot of help it was when, having put the question to her, I was told they were clients she received in rotation. . . . So you live by prostitution, I said. We live by prostitution, she said" (43). He asks to be fed parsnips. It is a quid pro quo, though how it is hard to say. He puts up with the grunts, he gets parsnips.

One day Lulu announces that she is pregnant, "by me of all people!" (44). With the approach of the child, her plaguing him with "our child" and exhibiting her belly, he thinks of abandoning her, but dreads the winter. "What finished me was the birth" (44). To shut out the wailing of the mother, he forces his exit through the jammed hallway, expelling himself from the house. As it happens it was never a certified marriage, a union, rather, in spite of all. Regret in the closure. "I could have done with other loves perhaps. But there it is, either you love or you don't" (45).

It would seem that two stories are conflated in *The Expelled*, the memory of being thrown out of the family house, and the memory of a time he spent with a cabman looking for a place to stay; or possibly every eviction from charitable institutions brings back that first expulsion from the family home, when he was thrown down the front steps on which he had played as a child. They hurled his hat after him, perhaps out of consideration; it covered the pustule on the top of his skull. The window to his room was "outrageously open. A thorough cleansing was in full swing. In a few hours they would close the window, draw the curtains and spray the whole place with disinfectant. I knew them. I would have gladly died in that house."[11] His offense, it is intimated, was a hardening asociability, a keeping to his room, a metamorphosis, a keeping to his bed in the middle of his room so as to shun the window. "I felt ill at ease with all this air about me" (49).

As if in answer to our puzzlement, he describes his gait, a pronounced duck walk. It must have had his classmates in stitches. He could not correct it, and conjectures its cause to be the frequent befouling of his pants when a schoolboy and his resistance to doing anything about it. This inclination to walk beshitted, legs stiff and wide apart, disposed him to being "sour and mistrustful" (51). But we see it is blarney, concocted for the hell of it or to wink at our detective ways. "[T]he fog won't lift" (51) on the wherefores of his being a misfit.

Upon setting forth he just avoids crushing a child "wearing a little harness . . . with little bells" (51) but knocks down "an old lady covered with spangles and lace." "[A]ll their foul little happiness" (52), he reflects of the ubiquitous parents, a crowd of them involving him in their anxious caretaking, and he waddles off thinking that "[t]hey never lynch children, babies, no matter what they do they are whitewashed in advance" (52), and cursing that the old lady didn't break a femur.

He takes refuge in a horse-drawn cab caught in the traffic of a funeral, and is roused from a doze by the cabman. In explaining how it is that he has a little money in his pocket and could afford hiring the cab, it becomes clear that a number of years have lapsed between his expulsion from his home and the adventure with the cabman. He treats the man to lunch, listens to the story of his hard life, and he in turn describes his situation. By "situation," he means to imply his being at a loss about living, his life gone adrift. The cabman understands only that he has lost his room and seeks another. They fruitlessly spend the waning winter day checking out rooms, the cabman whistling on the box. Our man recalls the pleasure of assisting in lighting the two oil lamps on the cab and watching the flames burn steady and snug in their little shelters. He allows the touching detail to stand, and juxtaposes it to the pathos of the horse's hard life, prohibited from eating and drinking until stabled, and muzzled to prevent him receiving scraps from passersby.

After treating his friend to drinks, he is invited to spend the night with him and his wife. He remembers the cabman's wife's unease, and that by his own insistence it was agreed that he would sleep in the stable below. During the night, he says, "I was seized, then abandoned, by the desire to set fire to the stable" (59). The wakeful horse appears to distrust him. He is made uneasy by its restlessness and spends the latter part of the night in the cab. At dawn, the stable door being locked, he leaves by way of a window, expelling himself with some difficulty. He leaves a banknote, "Weakness" (59), but on second thought pockets it. "The horse was still at the window" (60) watching him. And that's the story.

The illogicality, the shape of the narrative, the importance of the horse—there is no pinning it down—the unaccountably nasty; the thought, "let me wipe it first, it stinks of humanity"; the plausibility, indeed, of his having become sour and suspicious from too much shitting in his pants. He says he doesn't know why he told this story. The long face of the horse had lodged in his dreams. There it is whenever he gives a kick to a dilapidated pigsty, during his searches for shelter. He says in conclusion, "I could just as well have told another [story]. Perhaps some other time I'll be able to tell another. Living souls, you will see how alike they are" (60): as aimless and unfit for living as the narrator.

The narrator of *The End* also begins with his eviction from a charitable institution. Three women forcibly dress him. He kicks over a chair in angry protest. Aside from the clothes of a dead man that he has been stuffed into, he is given the usual allotment of money to get a start. An administrator of the institution smiles at his newly acquired tractability. He will reform himself. He pleads his old age. He is given leave to wait out the rain. Expelled from the grounds, the charitable institution's garden, under a late sun, he passes a mother and son walking together. The son points in wonder at the sky's sudden brightness. "Fuck off, she said."[12] It is not his first eviction from such places. The funny juxtaposition solidifies our loyalty to the deadbeat.

Off he goes not knowing where he is going into unfamiliar streets. "My appearance still made people laugh, with that hearty jovial laugh so good for the health" (81), likely alluding to his duck waddle; and though he solves the problem of tipping his hat without exposing his pustule, doors of houses where rooms are to let are slammed in his face. Finally he rents a basement from a woman who is "not alarm[ed]" by his "oddities" (83).

He wishes to be left alone to lounge on his bed or to sit on a chair beside the basement window. He purchases a crocus, which withers, and seems to prefer the plant that way. Something damns him, a wrong—birth, probably. He wants an undisturbed, dark, quiet place. Murmurs are okay, not sharp sounds like the cries of newsboys, but muffled, indistinguishable sounds. He imagines a young girl singing somewhere above him. We see why he continuously shat and bepissed his pants when a child. Life came entirely on "their" terms. He is bitter, angry, sardonic, resigned, hopeless. His life has been a repetition of ejections. He would doze to the inaudible murmurings above him, imagines it a lullaby, and dreams that a little girl with red hair in two long braids came to visit him. Perhaps a policeman and afterward a priest did. Under suspicion, patronized, cozened—his landlady cozens him. She gives him a twenty-five percent reduction for six months rent in advance and disappears. She had been caretaker while the owner was away. Our hero is expelled by the owner, who claims to need the basement for his pig.

He sleeps in a field on a heap of dung. He is thrown off three buses in an effort to get back to the city. He sits by the roadside drying his clothes in the sun. He mentions catching sight of his son.

> He was striding along with a briefcase under his arm. He took off his hat and bowed and I saw he was as bald as a coot. I was almost certain it was he. I turned round to gaze after him. He went bustling along on his duck feet, bowing and scraping and flourishing his hat left and right. The insufferable son of a bitch. (87)

But why grant his son his own duck walk, a son who does not appear to have his pustule? Perhaps it is a picture of the man "they" would have him be, useful, accommodating, freshened and disinfected. "[E]nough vile parrot I'll kill you."[13]

Midway on his hapless drift to death there is a pause. He stays with someone who is just managing to scrape by selling seawrack and sand with the help of an old donkey, and sheltering in a cave. The narrator smiles at the recollection and embroiders the scene,

> But to my amazement I got up on the ass and off we went, in the shade of the red chestnuts springing from the sidewalk. . . . The little boys jeered and threw stones, but their aim was poor, for they only hit me once, on the hat. A policeman stopped us and accused us of disturbing the peace. . . . We followed the quiet, dust-white inland roads with their hedges of hawthorn and fuchsia and their footpaths fringed with wild grass and daisies. Night fell. The ass carried me right to the mouth of the cave, for in the dark I could not have found my way down the path winding steeply to the sea. Then he climbed back to his pasture. (88)

This has a lovely simplicity. Salvation is to be found in never having been born. The cave-womb suggestion is played on a little further. Even in that shelter, or especially, he feels the sea pressing on him, "its splashing and heaving, its tides and general convulsiveness" (89), the pressure of ejection. His acquaintance remains a shadow figure, an idea perhaps of comradeship, but too little, too late. "You will always find me here . . . if you ever need me. Ah people. He gave me his knife" (89), surely the knife in the fairy tale his father told him.

He makes a shelter of a doorless, windowless shed filthy with excrement, condoms, and vomit. He makes a bed of ferns and slowly starves on it. The chance udder of a cow revives him. Events become fantastic. An invisible narrator is felt behind the persona, inventive, there and not there, yet separate, moving the story to an end he is working out, seeking, while our man decays in rags and filth on a sunny street corner, begging. This he contrives to do without too much disgusting passersby with the contrivance of a board jutting far enough from his body for coins to be proffered without touching him. He strews it with wild growing things that come his way, and so he survives, watching the sky, jostled by street urchins, scratching himself. Once he is made the object of oratory:

> Look at this down and out, he vociferated, this leftover. . . . It never enters your head . . . that your charity is a crime, an incentive to slavery. . . . Take a good look at this living corpse. You may

say it's his own fault. Ask him if it's his own fault. . . . Do you hear
me, you crucified bastard! cried the orator. (94–95)

And occasionally dogs would piss on his trouser leg.

At one point the invisible narrator intrudes. Our man has just
told us that his shed (this is news) is on a private estate along
the river. He begins to dilate on the view from the shed, build-
ings, steeples, a parade ground, and makes an abrupt stop. "[N]o,
I can't" (95), and starts again. This time it is an abandoned
estate along the river. The shed (perhaps our man adopted a different one) has a boat. He sleeps within it, having removed the
thwarts. He applies ingenuity to guard himself against water
rats. Again the narrator intrudes, mocking his own invention,
his persona's carpentry. Without tools, and with boards evidently
ubiquitous, he makes a coffin of his boat, fashioning a tight-fit-
ting cover in which he pierces a small hole. There he lies, en-
wombed in owl-light, listening to the sounds of water.

> As for my needs, they had dwindled as it were to my dimensions
> and become, if I may say so, of so exquisite a quality as to exclude
> all thought of succour. To know I had a being, however faint and
> false, outside of me, had once had the power to stir my heart. You
> become unsociable, it's inevitable. It's enough to make you
> wonder sometimes if you are on the right planet. (97)

He had come to feel that the "he" the "they" addressed wasn't he.
"There you are still between the two murmurs" (97)—their re-
quests/demands and his replies. "[I]t must be the same old song
as ever, but Christ you wouldn't think so" (97).

This feeling of being an "I" that is the real me, the other a
sham, is a revelation for the reader. It is the search and struggle
of a later narrator as determined to be that unnamable self as
K. to reach the Castle. "There were times when I wanted to push
away the lid and get out of the boat and couldn't, I was so indo-
lent and weak, so content deep down where I was. I felt them
hard upon me, the icy, tumultuous streets, the terrifying faces,
the noises that slash, pierce, claw, bruise" (97–98). Here we have
the stance of the artist towards his piece of flotsam, and more
than a glimpse of the hardening associability, the metamorphosis, that set him adrift.

His mind drifts. He imagines himself floating downriver into the bay, remembers standing on the heights overlooking the bay with his father. He imagines the tide carrying him out to sea—perhaps it is the delirium of death; this will happen to Malone in a later narrative. He has chained himself to the boat. He opens a plughole in the floorboards. "Back now in the stern-sheets, my legs stretched out, my back well propped against the sack stuffed with grass I used as a cushion, I swallowed my calmative" (99). Perhaps the only real calmative is a painless suicide. But the invisible narrator, who stands behind this one, he of *The Calmative*, cannot take his own life. The story of *The End* is his wish-fulfillment, which he breaks into at the end when he speaks directly and not through his character. "The memory came faint and cold of the story I might have told, a story in the likeness of my life, I mean without the courage to end or the strength to go on" (99).

Ventriloquized voices begin the narrative of *The Calmative*, perhaps trial runs to find his next story. He is damned to live on through his stories. "I'm too frightened this evening to listen to myself rot. . . . So I'll tell myself a story, I'll try and tell myself another story, to try and calm myself."[14] The prelude to his walking the earth again in search of material for his stories portrays the writer's hell, the cold grave of living on, dead to life, and generating stories to escape the consciousness of being deathlike.

Once again he walks in the fields toward the ramparts of his childhood town. His adventure will prove to be a dream, a dreamlike story in which he, the teller, feels and seems to be the object of somebody else's story. As the adventure continues the anguish becomes more intense and more precise. Everything is imaginary: he cannot get out of a story he may be thinking; or, he may be a character in a story someone else is thinking.

A comedian is telling funny stories to an enraptured audience outside the ramparts. Improbably, it is hardly dawn. He too, like the audience, wants to feel caught up and concentrated in the anticipation of a story, like the one his father told him when a boy about the lighthouse keeper's son who swam with a knife in his teeth after a shark. Above all he wants to be freed, he wants a story to end all stories, "to vanish in the havoc of its images" (63)—and be released, transformed into unthinkable newness:

the subjective self he was before birth and the fall into unconsciousness.

He enters the empty noiseless city wearing his father's greatcoat round his withered body, its skirts scraping the ground, and follows the river to the harbor. "I might slip unnoticed aboard a freighter outward bound . . . perhaps even a year or two, in the sun. . . . And without going that far it would be a sad state of affairs if in that unscandalizable throng I couldn't achieve a little encounter that would calm me a little" (65).

A boy holding a goat by the horn stands looking at him, silently, in rags, without fear or revulsion, one of the harbor guttersnipes. What will the narrator make of this? What needs has he? Who is it that thinks, "Can this base thought be mine?" (66). The boy presses up against him and offers him a penny sweet. Our hero solicits, and ashamed, covers his face. The boy gives him the candy and leaves. The narrator passes into reveries about the boy, and professes to consider the pale alternative of sniffing and even tasting the goat's dung.

Is it all for the sake of the respite that the narrator would lose himself in a story, the story being the calmative, the spentness, the torpor? But this story is a nightmare with a revelation, and the old man knows what it is. It is the revelation that an old, old man is telling a story in which he is the subject of the same story told by an identical old man who is the subject of the same story . . . in a sequence receding out of view like a great caravan crossing a desert. There is no way out and there is no end.

Feeling watched as he retraces his path through the city, he enters a church to take cover. "The brilliantly lit nave appeared deserted" (68). Our man walks about apprehensively. Suddenly the organ booms close to where he is standing. Fleeing at top speed, he mistakes a side-aisle door for the exit and mounts a spiral staircase "like one hotly pursued by a homicidal maniac" (68). He moves out onto the parapet below the church dome with the open nave below, gingerly, flattened against the wall, and meets a man revolving from the opposite direction. The man sidles back to where he had come from and then reappears on the opposite side of the parapet descending the stairwell with a little girl. About this episode, one can only repeat W. S. Merwin's comment about certain experiences being "objects of contemplation more than of analysis."[15] Still, the hints of Joseph K. in the cathedral chapter of *The Trial* are unmistakable. There can be no acquittal because there is no one to grant it. There are only stories, some with the power to sedate.

Back in the street he discovers himself to be lost. He is fearful, yet desperate to inquire of anyone, "Excuse me your honour, the Shepherds' Gate for the love of God!" (71). The city is as deserted as it was when he entered, only now it is the middle of the night, a contradiction plausible to the persona who discovers himself in a waking nightmare, or in somebody else's dream, a subject in his own dream, an object in another's. Who is speaking and in whose skull? Does what happens happen? It is all coming from behind him, everything he sees is moving in his direction. Is it possible to add anything? As an object, his physical pains are not his.

Although gliding as on rollers toward someone ahead of him, frantic to inquire the way out, he worries about disgusting the man with too sudden a sight of himself. However, the unknown person fails to see him. "I might as well not have existed. But what about the sweet? A light! I cried" (71). The allusions are funny: the indiscreet Gregor, all too visible; the unique sweetness of the goat boy's goat's turd—I taste, therefore I *do* exist—the cry for light. These associations and probably many others dispose us to the whims of the author chuckling behind the surface events.

His next encounter ought to comfort him. A man sits beside him on a stone bench and claims to be waiting for a hotel to make a room available. Our man is not only seen, he is asked to tell the story of his life. The stranger has a story and he tells it. We learn only about a Pauline he intends to abandon for someone else. Then it's our man's turn, who is prodded. "Are thighs much in your thoughts, he said, arses, cunts and environs? I didn't follow. No more erections naturally, he said. Erections? I said. The penis, he said, you know what the penis is" (73), and goes on marveling at the mystery of engorgement and tumefaction. Our man inquires after Pauline. "But what will become of her? I said. . . . She will grow old, he said with tranquil assurance, slowly at first, then faster and faster, in pain and bitterness, pulling the devil by the tail" (73). Our man confides the homicidal thought of stabbing him and looks for the signs in the face gone chalky.

Instead the stranger opens a black bag full of glittering vials and, displaying one, suddenly grabs our man by the back of the neck and presses up against him. Some act with murmuring caresses transpires. Passion spent, the man transacts a kiss in the middle of his forehead in exchange for one of his vials.

Our man sets off again, but with his pains returned, and his familiar duck walk. "To think that in a moment all will be said, all to do again" (75). A thought kept at bay grows in him, for mercy. He imagines a child's smile, and falls to his knees "as cattle do" (76) at slaughter, or is it in prayer as the oxen do at the Nativity? "But up with me again and back on the way that was not mine" (76), he reflects, despairing to be the old man despairing in someone else's story. "But in vain I raised without hope my eyes to the sky to look for the Bears. For the light I stepped in put out the stars" (76–77), ending on the pathos of there being no exit for him, as there was for Dante.

Molloy and Malone are not quite discernible in the *Nouvelles*, which open the way to them. Beckett's mature vision of life is not clear enough in the stories to help us understand Molloy's aesthetics for survival, Malone's heroism, and the Unnamable's lucidity, though the characters in the *Nouvelles* behave as if it were clear. I do not mean that the characters in the *Nouvelles* would understand Molloy's vision of existence as shadow-show, and of life as world collapsing endlessly—timeless, pointless, endless decay, eternally recurring—but they implicitly understand that living requires an exoskeleton, the façade existence, and that those subject to catastrophe are not to blame for not being able to turn into lobsters. They can do nothing about it; from the beginning, they have no way or will to survive. One could say that in *First Love*, the youth is merely eccentric; in *The Expelled*, he appears schizophrenic; in *The End*, hapless.

The Calmative introduces the plight of the writer who depends on stories to give him a semblance of being, and who, though in despair, would not change his death-in-life existence for ordinary life if he could. Yet stories provide a poor substitute for life—"But can that be called a life which vanishes when the subject is changed?" (*The Unnamable* 353)—and a worse affliction after the respite from self that stories provide. Why then cannot the writer be silent about life? What compels him to write? Beckett takes hold of these questions, born out of the *Nouvelles*, and pursues them relentlessly throughout his oeuvre. As stories related by the narrator of *The Calmative*, *First Love* and *The Expelled* may be told to exorcise disturbing memories; the third, *The End*, has behind it the wish to explain, and implicit in the explanation, prayer—the narrator's prayer to make an end of himself, find quittance in the only real calmative possible.

It is a wish-fulfillment. Death is not, cannot be the intention of the hero of *The Calmative*. For his is an absurd existence: he stands as an invisible author behind the character-narrators in the stories these fictional heroes tell, while at the same time he is aware of his own fictional status. He "knows" that his story is being told while he narrates. His fate determines the fate of his characters. His consciousness of his fictional status symbolizes their sense of being at a loss about how to live among others who believe in the reality of their existences. They can do nothing for themselves that matters. They have abandoned their names. Names are part of the entrapment, the confiscation of self by others—by contact, by using their language, by being objectified, by being his-her-their answers to the question, who am I, and so becoming irretrievably stifled behind one's social mask.

Can we think of the stories of *The Calmative* narrator as efforts to speak with his submerged voice of a time before his fall into self-consciousness, when he was all in all himself, an empty mind at peace? This, in Thomas J. Cousineau's reading (1999) of *The Unnamable*, would be to retrieve his authentic desire. Stories, then, are efforts to recover one's true subjective being and so answer the question, who am I? The narrator of *The Calmative* creates characters with crippled consciousnesses, aimless and angry, out of a compulsion to sedate his pain by massaging the wound of his birth.

By contrast, his existence depends on the continued interest of the unknown author of his own story—on the wit of his play with things as they come along, on the situations he invents ad hoc, on the originality of his improvisation—on his performance.

He must go on, incapable of really knowing whether he's the author or a character in the story being told; for he wants to believe that he has an existence, and dreads not knowing, but prefers the nightmare of fictional status to real life. He does not want the author to cut him off as a failed or finished work; he does not want real existence. Dread keeps him going: dread of the words of another's narrative never ending, and dread of their ending, and the dread of his never being able to know he exists. Losing himself in telling a story is his only calmative— the only calmative possible. Articulation is the only real power we have.

This new stance of the author, who stands behind his character, who's himself an author of stories, but uncertain whether inventor or invented, conscious of being cut off from reality and surrounded by the illusions he substitutes, perhaps a fictitious being shaping his own existence, yet nevertheless driven to prove his own self-presence, opened the way for Beckett to the trilogy.[16]

Life as unspeakable, the predicate for becoming social misfits in the *Nouvelles*, is the continuous rallying cry to the Unnamable's indefatigable dodging:

> [A]nd little by little the old problem will raise its horrid head, how to live, with their kind of life, for a single second, young or old. . . . with their billions of quick, their trillions of dead, that's not enough for them, I too must contribute my little convulsion, mewl, howl, gasp and rattle, loving my neighbour and blessed with reason. But what is the right manner, I don't know. It is they who dictate this torrent of balls. . . . the same old sour teachings I can't change a tittle of (334–35). This catechist's tongue, honeyed and perfidious, is the only one they know (356). I have to puke my heart out too, spew it up whole along with the rest of the vomit, it's then at last I'll look as if I mean what I'm saying (335–36). Orders, prayers, threats, praise, reproach, reasons. . . . I'll die in the lower third, bowed down with years and impositions, four foot tall again, like when I had a future. . . . And I'll fall down dead, worn out by the rudiments (337). Someone has therefore something to say to me. But never the least news concerning me (336). Do they believe I believe it is I who am speaking? . . . They'll never get the better of my stupidity (345–46). It's this hunt that is tiring, this unending being at bay (346). In their shoes I'd be con-

tent with my knowing what I know, I'd demand no more of me than to know that what I hear is not the innocent and necessary sound of dumb things constrained to endure, but the terror-stricken babble of the condemned to silence (354). [T]hey say I don't want it either, don't want peace, after all perhaps they're right, how could I want it, what is it, they say I suffer, perhaps they're right, and that I'd feel better if I did this, said that, if my body stirred, if my head understood, if they went silent and departed, perhaps they're right, how would I know about these things, how would I understand what they're talking about, I'll never stir, never speak, they'll never go silent, never depart, they'll never catch me, never stop trying, that's that, I'm listening (381). It will make no difference. Where I am there is no one but me, who am not. (355)

The idea that the misfits of the *Nouvelles* are searching for a self, prelinguistic, uncontaminated by existence, is mentioned in *The End*: "To know I had a being, however faint and false, outside of me, had once had the power to stir my heart. You become unsociable, it's inevitable" (97). This idea of a search for the true self, touched upon in the *Nouvelles* as the impetus to a quest involving a metamorphosis from ordinary to misfit, cuts like a Rabelaisian scythe through the trilogy, where the quest for the real "I" parodically strips away all that which informs the minds of ordinary people. And this searching for self brings to mind a fairy tale, the one about the princess who will not let the enamoured dragon near her until it sheds a layer of skin—it is too horny and rough. This the dragon does with great pain. Another layer is requested, and another, excruciating to the dragon, who finally out of its last agony, steps forth as a prince. The Unnamable—who represents in one guise the fictional status of Beckett himself as author—suspects that there is no way to liberate the prince whom he would believe is inside him. Needing to know may be the deepest motive of the creative drive.

The trilogy, Chapters 2–4:
A Strange Justice

Prelude to the trilogy:
A Strange Justice

1

Here I pose the problem of Samuel Beckett's artistic stance in the celebrated trilogy and how his governing ideas operate. Beckett wrote the novels in French in the late 1940s, *Molloy* and *Malone Dies* appearing in 1951, *The Unnamable* in 1953, and translated them into English himself in the mid-1950s.[1]

All three are monologues, although *Molloy* has the peculiarity of being two monologues, two fictional recountings of the invention of Molloy. The second, Moran's, describes the frantic joy ride into dispossession and transformation to a state of being resembling that of Molloy. Molloy, apostle of irreverence and blasphemy, "had [he] only the little finger to raise to be wafted straight to Abraham's bosom [he'd] tell him to stick it up."[2] These words, from Beckett's *How It Is* (1961), precisely convey Molloy's disaffection with the scheme of things, a disgust requiring strategies for survival on his own terms. The chief danger to him lies in the pressure of conscience that would turn Molloy into "the inexpugnable" (*The Unnamable* 347) personality of a type like Moran, householder and sadist.

The trilogy is a world in which one either participates in the grand narrative of Guilt, Redemption, Reward and Punishment, or makes up one's own stories, fictionalizing self in order to avoid being fictionalized. Speculation on the functions of stories and the origins of the creative drive progress through the monologues to an overriding question: is it possible, since one must use language, to escape the fate of programmed thinking? How speak lines that are not scripted, grounded in conscience, watered with tears of remorse? "[A]ll it needs is preaching on, to become a living torch, screams included" (361) says the Unnamable, abjuring his right to be born. Precisely the dying Malone's view of his situation: caught up by the mad wish to know, to remember his transgressions, and yet struggling time and again not to remember, to leave stocktakings to this year's crop of the damned. Valiantly striving to be spewed out as unreclaimable—that's Malone. Whirled about in a vortex without a center, no gravity, an addendum to Dante's hell, rallying on futilely—is he damned for spiritual suicide, or for striving after a strange justice?

The struggle is stripped to its most basic in *The Unnamable*: no props, no stage, no space whatsoever, just the narrator's wits versus the divine ventriloquist, fought out in the antechamber of rebirth in the heated expectation of conception. Personal identity is the issue, the striving to assert it in an eternally recurring circuit of life and death, in which a subject's wriggle may be the only variable. How is one to endure, and should the reader champion such courage, in light of this perception of the situation?

I suggest at the outset one answer to this question which is based on a continuous impression about *The Unnamable* and the spiritual excitement to which it gives rise. Here I explore the connection between the text and oral testimonies of survivors of the Holocaust, making use of Maurice Blanchot's *The Writing of the Disaster* (1986) to draw out the suggestive correspondences.

Molloy and Malone, to whom life is like a death camp, defy the creator/commandant, cost them what it may. They cannot understand the compromised ways of ordinary people and how such people can be possible. The Unnamable narrator has tasted existence and resists being reborn out of the ashes. This perception of his situation—inevitable perhaps to an author who survived the German occupation hiding in a small town in southern France that was also a sanctuary for Jews—raises a subtextual problem I cannot satisfactorily answer. Moran is a killer, Gestapo it is hinted, taking orders from one Youdi. Why show clemency by transforming hysteria and dispossession into our valorous Molloy, and why assign Moran's master a Jewish name?

2

Molloy is a fugitive; his fugitive life is his subject—his going on with his life in face of the world—a going on, that is, until existence cannot be accommodated. His toughness and staying power (the same is even more true for Malone and the Unnamable) is "a sort of mighty if preposterous moral deed," as Malcolm Lowry describes the hero of *Under the Volcano.*[3]

Molloy's memoir has nothing to do with real memory, because memory for him is a tool for invention. His memoir begins by his talking to himself of himself through the first sketchings of what might be a story, showing in the process his artistic freedom in regard to his own story. The social worker is described as a fat woman, "a big fat woman dressed in black, or rather in mauve" (23). Or rather white? He changes details as he goes along in order to keep memory at bay.

"It is in the tranquillity of decomposition that I remember the long confused emotion which was my life, and that I judge it" (25). No. What he judges, lying in his mother's bed "in the tranquillity of decomposition," is all human life. Decomposing in bed is not escaping. Just existing is torture, just being is crying out. "Let me cry out then, it's said to be good for you. Yes, let me cry out, this time, then another time perhaps, then perhaps a last time" (25). But there can be no relief. "The shadow in the end is no better than the substance" (26). The crying out is even more frantic in the unborn Unnamable at the prospect of being birthed. Molloy refers to himself as a survivor among corpses. "Yes, there is no denying it, any longer, it is not you who are dead, but all the others. So you get up and go to your mother, who thinks she is alive. That's my impression" (27).

Suicide is not an option. He may have mystical moments of bleeding out (one, anyway, which must stand for the occasional) when he feels released from "that sealed jar to which I owed my being so well preserved"—deadpan, it's probably blarney—"and I filled with roots and tame stems for example" (49). He speaks of hearing sounds, "pure sounds, free of all meaning" (50), something like distant music. One might surmise that these feelings, intimations, keep him going. When he sets out to open a wrist and then decides against it, he says, "So much for that. And backsliding has always depressed me" (61). He is at that moment leaning against a wall and resting at a vertical angle owing to a stiff leg. Opening a wrist would be literally backsliding down the wall.

Several times Moran mutters to himself, "He asked for a report, he'll get his report" (120). Moran's report to Youdi is a form of insubordination. It is not an agent's report but a writer's. Why was the mission a failure? In point of fact Moran had become disabled, crippled, and his son had abandoned him. Like *The Calmative*, the Moran narrative presents the writer's own "story" as well as the story he's creating. Genesis as "a crumbling, a frenzied collapsing of all that had always protected me from all I was always condemned to be." Then, "all darkness and bulk, with a noise like the grinding of stones, then suddenly as soft as water flowing" (148). This, in other words, is to say that he fails his assigned mission because he submits to the writer's dispossession of self.

Beckett may have modeled Moran and Molloy after the two types of servants Mr. Knott likes to have look after him in the earlier novel *Watt*: the one, "small fat seedy shabby juicy or oily bandylegged potbellied potbottomed" and the other, "big bony seedy shabby haggard knockkneed rottentoothed rednosed."[4]

Malone's plan, "to live, and cause to live, at last, to play at last and die alive" (209), is to die free of the past, "misted and smeared with the filth of years" (198). Pulling off a synchrony of his death with that of his character, he would be in control, parodically on his terms—"alive." He has set his life against the pressures to conform, intending to live without "poltroonery" (189). But it is impossible for Malone to know himself, or whether there is a self that is not performance—performance (like the Unnamable's) of a consciousness desperately doubting its own existence while doggedly hating and resisting human life. Going another step, the Unnamable refuses to be, in the Christian ethos, one of the sheep, the shepherd's pet—no matter how black.

2
Inventing Molloy

M olloy begins by announcing that he is a writer, that he is in his mother's room, and that there will be two further narratives in addition to the one he is writing. As for his situation, inhabiting his deceased mother's room, "I sleep in her bed. I piss and shit in her pot. I have taken her place. I must resemble her more and more. All I need now is a son" (7). This may be a good punch line to a joke, but it turns out to be a likely reason for Molloy's lifelong circling about his mother. Perhaps he had a son, a son who is also his brother.

Who is this Molloy who announces that there will be three narratives? Malone speaks of him as his fictive creation, and Molloy sounds like Malone when he says in frustration at not being able to describe the themes of the three stories, "for it is one, in a sense." "It's my fault" (8). Instantly he catches himself up, "Fault? That was the word. But what fault?" (8). One can surmise that the word came out inadvertently; the mystery of three in one brought it forth. Submergence in language, which depends upon an entire structure of perceptions generated by social experience and religious beliefs, made it inescapable. Fault, or guilt, to Malone is an outrage perpetrated by the diligent and edified of God's creatures, perhaps foreordained by Him out of wickedness. Malone says, "well I'll be buggered" (225) when the notion of fault slips in. These slips he cannot help. He, too, is infected by "the gonococcus in the folds of the prostrate" (197). He is in perpetual war against the poisonous feeling of guilt. Even more extreme, the Unnamable strives in valiant futility for freedom within the belly of being itself.

45

In professing his past to be a blur—in slipping the chains of memory, Molloy, in essence, describes his degree of freedom from guilt. He reads what he has written, the beginning of a fictional memoir. His improvisation and storytelling about two characters named A and C illustrate his chief tactic of survival. Molloy continuously reinvents himself through his stories, just as he improvises in his invention of C, in order to exist only in a time present, with no past, no memories. Without memory—guilt—he would be unavailable to the grand narrative, and fortified in his invincible repugnance for its hooks. The continuous danger of his becoming ensnared stimulates his invention.

The memoir begins with Molloy flattened on a rock observing two men in greatcoats walking toward each other, two wayfaring strangers on a country road, one tall, the other short. Revision: Or perhaps they know each other. They meet and exchange a few words, A then returning to town, leaving C, who becomes the object of Molloy's speculation—imagining what C sees, looking with him through the lens of his emotions. Sketching this imagined landscape pleases Molloy.

He portrays an old, solitary, lonely man uncertain and apprehensive in the gathering night, carrying a stick. Molloy broadens his sketch. C is now shaping into a character who carries a stout stick because he is fearful. Molloy suggests that C's "anxiety" is not necessarily his, but the author's, as it were, "overtaking him" (10). In a word, he indicates a crude motive for his working-up C: the discharging of his own anxiety. Anxiety, in *Molloy* as in the trilogy as a whole, is formulaic; it manifests susceptibility to memory and fear of becoming translated into the grand narrative. And as such, it fuels the creative drive. Without storytelling, there can be no striving for freedom. But what value freedom if realized only as a great refusal?

> [F]ree, yes, I don't know what that means but it's the word I mean to use, free to do what, to do nothing, to know, but what, the laws of the mind perhaps, of my mind, that for example water rises in proportion as it drowns you and that you would do better, at least no worse, to obliterate texts than to blacken margins, to fill in the holes of words till all is blank and flat and the whole ghastly business looks like what is, senseless, speechless, issueless misery. (13)

Why endure on the life-support of stories?

The great pull, like a vortex in Molloy's life, the repository of his past, the source of his guilt, is mother. She is the symbol of all that necessitates Molloy's continual reinvention of self: Mother Molloy as the cage that would catch up to its bird, otherwise free, though hobbling on crutches. Molloy must go there so as to sniff around the place where the crime of birth occurred, as if there were a way out of the fate of being himself, a loophole.

Molloy pictures for us the generic visit in extravagant parody. The parody rides on a disgust and rage that at the same time are diffused by it. He says that he tried to train his mother to understand him by a series of knocks on her skull. She knew him by his smell, but her mind was gone, like her sight and hearing. He says he called her Mag in order to pronounce the Ma while spitting on it at the same time. He took her money, but always after attempting to pound this into her skull, and never without rattling the bills under her nose and jamming them into her mouth. Perhaps conation comes closest to explaining his periodic need to visit her. "First taste of the shit" (16), he says.

> My mother. I don't think too harshly of her. I know she did all she could not to have me, except of course the one thing, and if she never succeeded in getting me unstuck, it was fate that earmarked me for less compassionate sewers. But it [her attempts to abort him] was well-meant and that's enough for me. No it is not enough for me, but I give her credit, though she is my mother, for what she tried to do for me. And I forgive her for having jostled me a little in the first months [trying to unstick him, no doubt] and spoiled the only endurable, just endurable, period of my enormous history. (18)

This prelude to the journey home has one further revelation:

> And if ever I'm reduced to looking for a meaning to my life, you never can tell, it's in that old mess I'll stick my nose to begin with, the mess of that poor old uniparous whore and myself the last of my foul brood, neither man nor beast. I should add, before I get down to the facts, you'd swear they were facts, of that distant summer afternoon, that with this deaf blind impotent mad old woman, who called me Dan [his father's name] and whom I called Mag, and with her alone, I—no, I can't say it. (19)

This last clarification, as if dredged up, heavily hinting at incest, would explain "uniparous whore and myself the last of my foul brood." But is he the last? Has he a son/brother, and is it part of Beckett's contrivance to bring forth the son/brother in Moran? "Good. Now that we know where we're going, let's go there" (19), chirps Molloy.

His first adventure on the way to mother, having entered town and pausing to rest—leaned forward astride his bicycle dressed in his accustomed rags, his head on his arm, his stiff leg extended, his crutches balanced against the handlebars—is to be arrested for public indecency. He cannot resist playing with the absurd idea of his piteous fate—being dragged off to jail by a policeman in broad daylight. In the scene he sketches, Molloy dotingly imagines the daily interests of these ordinary townfolk and the great gulf that separates him from them. "[W]hat strain, as of hawsers about to snap? It's possible. Yes, I was straining towards those spurious deeps, their lying promise of gravity and peace, from all my old poisons I struggled towards them, safely bound. Under the blue sky, under the watchful gaze. Forgetful of my mother, set free from the act, merged in this alien hour, saying, Respite, respite" (21). Under the watchful gaze of the policeman, straining at the hawsers like Odysseus in the enchantment of the siren call, craving respite, release from the past, from his being birthed by his mother, from the fate of being birthed by that particular mother. This sort of impromptu is an effort to blow off the anxiety of his visit and gain emotional buoyancy. In this context of being born to a destiny, storytelling originates in the need to escape one's destiny through self-fictionalization.

Molloy's narrative consists of discrete parts. His encounters with people: policeman, sergeant, social worker, shepherd, Lousse, the charcoal burner. These are occasions for creating fiction for the sake of play; it is fiction for diversion, for escaping self, devouring time in clownishness and satire. His precise method of dealing with things and situations: riding a bicycle with a stiff leg, sucking stones, getting the best results kicking a supine foe while on crutches. These are like the former, fiction as play, means for keeping his mind off his predicament. And there are his meditations on his predicament as a member of the human race. This is the form of *Malone Dies*, play arresting meditation, controlling through fiction rather than wriggling in the control of another's fiction. How not to wriggle is the drama of *The Unnamable*, where the predicament is to keep from being born.

On being set again at liberty, Molloy pauses on his bicycle outside the windows of the guardhouse, enchanted by sight of his shadow cast on the white wall of the opposite building. "I began to play, gesticulating, waving my hat, moving my bicycle to and fro before me, blowing the horn, watching the wall. They were watching me through the bars, I felt their eyes upon me" (25–26). The meaning of shadow shows, fiction, "[a]n opiate for the life of the dead" (27), by which he means ordinary folk, occupy him as he meanders on his journey, shadow shows like God, and the Redeemer, and the Reward. Bemused, he describes a bargeman with a long white beard beating with a long pole a team of gentle donkeys towing the barge which is loaded with wood and nails for a carpenter. The scene becomes animated by Molloy's mood of parody: the horizon "burning with sulphur and phosphorus" (27), the big problem of life, "what saint to implore" (27).

His thoughts—on the way to a ditch where he stretches out and until he wakes at late morning observed by a shepherd— run on in a stream of consciousness. The connectors are associational. Living uncomatosed, without the shadow show of consolations, is like surviving in a death camp. He evokes the comparison: "the little night and its little lights, faint at first, then flaming and extinguished, now ravening, now fed, as fire by filth and martyrs" (28). What does it mean to be condemned to live? What can constitute prayer? Why keep going? How does he know that he is still alive? And does it matter? It will all repeat anyway.

Waking to find himself observed by a shepherd and his dog makes a good closure to a meditation on the grand narrative as the ultimate opiate. "Did he take me for a black sheep entangled in the brambles and was he waiting for an order from his master to drag me out?" (28). Yet this flock is headed for the slaughterer, he thinks, led by the shepherd to be slowly bled. There is the substance behind the shadow show. God is cruel, the saints are opiates, the flock is being led pacified to slaughter, it is all to recur again eternally, to live one must be comatosed, one cannot do without stories. But then why go on, why tease oneself with the fairy tale that there is something unimaginable, as yet to be understood? "You invent nothing, you think you are inventing, you think you are escaping, and all you do is stammer out your lesson, the remnants of a pensum one day got by heart and long forgotten, life without tears, as it is wept. To hell with it [the immemorial expiation] anyway" (32). There is no freedom, no loophole, no escaping the suspicion that all are the playthings of a sporting God. Still Molloy goes on.

Behind Molloy the character stands his author, and behind that Molloy, Malone, and behind him, the author of the trilogy, who has the supreme fiction in mind. At one point during the adventure with Lousse, Molloy becomes inhabited by the author of the trilogy; a stranger possesses him. Wakened by "a huge moon framed in the window" (39), Molloy begins thinking of a former life when he was occupied by study—astronomy, geology, anthropology, psychiatry—"Oh I've tried everything" (39). And with the words, "In the end it was magic that had the honour of my ruins" (39), he lapses into a trance. In what follows, Molloy's life and Beckett's art merge as the subject of the meditation, life and art in contradistinction to living and literature as they are familiarly understood. It is a distinction between living and writing within the unmediated experience of the devastation, and living and writing within a secure, value-oriented, and judgment-based world of denial. In the former there are only ruins without consolations. In the latter there is rectitude, a meaning to suffering, duties and ambitions. On the one hand, "the indestructible chaos of timeless things" (39), the monologues, *Godot*, *Endgame*, and *How It Is*; on the other, momentum, scenery, verisimilitude, purpose. The Beckettian world is devoid of mystery, the shadow show magic of meaning and reward. It is "a world collapsing endlessly, a frozen world, under a faint untroubled sky, enough to see by, yes, and frozen too" (40). No hint of the divine, no meaning to the immemorial expiation. "[B]ut here there are no loads, and the ground too, unfit for loads, and the light too, down towards an end it seems can never come. For what possible end to these wastes where true light never was, nor any upright thing, nor any true foundation, but only these leaning things, forever lapsing and crumbling away, beneath a sky without memory of morning or hope of night" (40). This is a prophetic seeing of Beckett/Molloy within the eye of the devastation, life as timeless, pointless, endless decay. "Yes, a world at an end, in spite of appearances, its end brought it forth, ending it began, it is clear enough?" (40). Existence as decay eternally recurring. "And I too am at an end, when I am there, my eyes close, my sufferings cease and I end, I wither as the living can not" (40).

Ordinary folk cannot endure reality. Knowing the creation for what it is, Molloy's fear of hope blighted ceases. But not altogether. "And if I went on listening to that far whisper, silent long since and which I still hear, I would learn still more, about this. But I will listen no longer, for the time being, to that far whisper, for I do not like it, I fear it" (40). What meaning to that far whisper? A tease? A summons? This is Malone's predicament, and a source of the Unnamable's ceaseless speculation. Is there a master? Or has a transformer been implanted at birth for a voice murmuring, implying meaning, intimating imperatives, which he cannot shut out? Is this also a motive for storytelling: to discover the meaning? Or to shut out the voice?

The motives for the creative drive are as many as the combinations in a slot machine. It depends on what is up and down between the body's pain, consciousness's state of autonomy, and the persuasiveness of the murmuring voice (conscience, or soul): to bear witness, to escape one's fate, to show life for what it is, to seek understanding, to appease. There are a dozen more. To escape tedium, to relieve by forgetting, to feel spiritually cleansed, to simulate life (something to do in place of living), to know where one has got to, to rise from the dead, to enjoy making something, to fill the want of companionship, to fill the want of love, to pray for love, to feel immune from vicissitudes, to presume to be in on the secret. And there are still more.

The narrative has the logic of a musical score. The jokes, set pieces, comic routines depend on his mood—on what is up and down in the psyche of Molloy in his battle with life—in combination with his situation in the narrative. The degree of play, wit, fertility of invention, surprise openings into a story, evolving of sentences that cascade into a series of punch lines, exhibit his admirable cheekiness, despite all.

The Lousse adventure—his enchantress drugs him in order to make a pet of him, a toothless old dog—tempts Molloy to fictionalize an amour: Molloy's one requited love affair with a woman, Ruth, Edith, he cannot remember.

> I would have preferred it seems to me an orifice less arid and roomy, that would have given me a higher opinion of love it seems to me. However. Twixt finger and thumb tis heaven in comparison. But love is no doubt above such base contingencies. And not when you are comfortable, but when your frantic member casts about for a rubbing-place, and the unction of a little mucous membrane, and meeting with none does not beat in retreat, but retains its tumefaction, it is then no doubt that true love comes to pass, and wings away, high above the tight fit and the loose. And when you add a little pedicure and massage, having nothing to do with the instant of bliss strictly speaking, then I feel no further doubt is justified, in this connexion. (58)

Such set piece comic routines as visiting mother, paean to true love, "[m]orning is the time to hide" (66), sucking stones with method, are nothing if not hygienic, a number of others in the trilogy—the love story of Hairy Mac and Sucky Molly, picnicking with Lady Pedal, the adventures of Mahood—are no less spiritually cleansing of the Moran in us.

Moran is the antithesis of Molloy, a massive, pear-shaped, violent man scarcely in control of an inner rage. In all respects he adheres to forms: his taking of Communion, punctuality in his meal-taking, the calculated pomposity in his deportment, exactitude in his household administration—every item of his possessions inventoried, everything in its place, and the key to every drawer, chest, and door on a ring in his pocket. He is a ponderous eater, a heavy presence. He does not laugh; what humor he has is sardonic. He dislikes people, en masse and in the particular. He dislikes animals with the exception of his bees and his hens, on which he dotes. Suspicious, always speaking in the imperative, he bullies his housekeeper without mercy. He tyrannizes his son, sanctioning the mental trashing and beatings of his thirteen-year-old as discipline. "It was not for nothing I had studied the old testament" (118).

Moran's report to Youdi begins with this essential picture of himself. He is to document his failure in "the Molloy affair" (98), the mission of the year before, when the messenger, Gaber, brought orders that he was to leave that night with his son to find Molloy. "[T]he poison I had just been given" (96), Moran comments in hindsight, anticipating the effect the orders had on his customary solidity. He accepts them as an imperative and hates Youdi for having dispatched them—precisely the relationship he has cultivated with his son, he sees.

> The thought that between my death and his own, ceasing for an instant from heaping curses on my memory, he might wonder, in a flash, whether I had not been right, that was enough for me, that repaid me for all the trouble I had taken and was still to take. He would answer in the negative, the first time, and resume his execrations. But the doubt would be sown. He would go back to it. That was how I reasoned. (110)

This could be Molloy's, Malone's, and the Unnamable's parable on the imperatives of a guilty conscience, this unending being at bay. The Molloy in Moran remains submerged while his official self proudly adheres to his master's call. He tracks and kills with a mystic's prescience for his quarry: can discern his victim through "the spray of phenomena" (111), "sense what course to follow, find peace in another's ludicrous distress" (110). His mystic trance is a getting down to business. He envisages life as a death camp. "All is dark, but with that simple darkness that follows like a balm upon the great dismemberings. From their places masses move, stark as laws. Masses of what? One does not ask" (110). Among them he discerns his prey; he can see himself bending down over him.

But Moran's genius and savor for the hunt do not work with Molloy. When he puts his mind to the business of apprehending Molloy, "I was nothing but uproar, bulk, rage, suffocation, effort unceasing, frenzied and vain" (113).

It is a strange report, detailing his efforts to rein in hysteria and follow orders. He rationalizes that he was an artist who had to risk going to pieces in order to perform his art, which he executed "tenderly." His work "would subsist, haunting the minds of men, when its miserable artisans should be no more" (114–15). Disdainful of his "weakness" (114), he proudly adds, "Ah those old craftsmen, their race is extinct and the mould broken" (115). The extended allusion to the systematic killing under Hitler is unmistakable. Moran scorns the thought that a man like him could "be haunted and possessed by chimeras" (114).

But Molloy is not just any victim. Moran has the presentiment of knowing him and of knowing Mother Molloy. It has been broadly hinted that Moran is Molloy's son and brother, which may be the business Molloy constantly refers to as remaining unsettled between him and his mother. Moran's finding out who he is, where he has got to, going home again, meeting himself along the way, contribute to a sense of disaster he cannot contain. He describes himself prowling his grounds and house restlessly. He cannot bring his mind to rest on Gaber's orders. He cannot recall them. He sees that he has made no preparations. He has no plan. He does not know what he is to do with Molloy once he finds him. "And yet there I was whistling away" (124).

His anger rises at Youdi and is displaced ferociously to his son, who does not want to go with him. The boy pleads illness. Moran applies an enema. The boy still refuses to go. Moran beats him with the handle of his umbrella. Trembling with rage, he rushes from his son's room, seizes an ax from the garden shed, and begins hacking furiously at an old garden block. He finds his son preparing for the journey and crying. Moran is in a spirited mood as they set forth. He is on a mission, following orders, and he is going to pieces, cutting his "sheet-anchors" (125) and marching forth with "bagpipes" (126) in hand to a dispossession he welcomes.

Why the two narrators? Are Molloy and Moran each the fiction of the other? Do they represent a dynamic in the creative process in which the official self gives way to the unofficial? The idea of abdication is underscored by two powerful speaking pictures: Moran's homicidal rage at an image of himself stalking Molloy, a double whose face he pulverizes, breaking his key ring and scattering his keys, and the image of the birthing of his new self visible below the water line, "swaying up slowly from the depths" (148–49).

Perhaps it is the most fitting punishment for Moran to be transformed into a tramp like Molloy. The synchrony of Molloy seeking his mother and Moran seeking Molloy lies in the mystery of brethren. It is hinted that both are Mother Molloy's progeny, both bearing "like a scurf of placenta, her stamp" (112). Moran's is a story of his "growing resignation to being dispossessed of self" (149). This newly evolving Moran fantasizes Molloy "a friend, and like a father to me" (162).

Moran's report to Youdi is incomplete. Molloy completes it by turning an account of failure into one of revolt, "of vagrancy and freedom" (132).

Moran's struggle grows into one primarily of resistance against the imperatives of his old self, "a roar, of triumph and distress" (166) as he undergoes his great inward metamorphosis and becomes, if not a son to Molloy, Molloy himself.

The two narratives of *Molloy* may also appear homiletic. The reader may hear in Moran's narrative his own voice whispering, "I have the soul of a collaborator. A Vichy government has set up headquarters in that soul. I have become exactly the kind of man I hate more than anything in the world. I keep a nice lawn and have never gotten a speeding ticket." In the Molloy narrative, the reader may hear his own voice murmuring, "In my deepest heart I believe in the rectitude of his private war with the world. His sense of engagement is a constant reminder of how much I have surrendered. I am not a man of principle, I am not a man of faith, I am not a man of action. I am a moral cripple."[5]

Molloy comments sardonically on the price one pays for burrowing into a niche for security. "[U]nfortunately there are other needs than that of rotting in peace" in one's "box" (75–76). The choice is between being harrowed by conscience into making a virtue of prudence, staying put and rotting, or surfacing to a life that is "a veritable calvary, with no limit to its stations and no hope of crucifixion" (78). It is a choice between spiritual death and ethical striving for the impossibility of justice.

Coda: Near a road somewhere in the multiverse, Moran collapses, scourged, abandoned, bereft, unrecognizable. Observing himself from his authorial lookout, Moran remarks that he was about to lose consciousness, "[a]nd though suffering a little from wind and cramps in the stomach I felt extraordinarily content, content with myself, almost elated, enchanted with my performance" (162–63). Surprise! How long had he suspected he was playacting at being an outcast in a cruel world? His boisterous mood announces Gaber before he spots him asleep on a tree-stump. That, he declares redundantly, "put a stop to these frolics" (163). Youdi's orders: "Moran . . . home, instanter" (163).

Was it all for nought? Had nothing essential changed? Gaber sees nothing, not the tiniest sign acknowledging a change in Moran. Moran, at his lookout, choreographs the scene. Two clowns, one in uniform with a notebook and pencil in hand, the other in rags, showing he cannot walk, displaying his enfeebled condition. Orders are repeated, Gaber departs, Moran totters after him grabbing his sleeve. Shaking with fear, he beseeches Gaber to relieve his mind. What is in store for him—what did Youdi say? The messenger does not understand; he would like a pint of lager. Moran pushed, falls, roars, implores, and then illumination. Gaber's face lights up. "He said to me, said Gaber, Gaber, he said—. Louder! I cried. He said to me, said Gaber, Gaber, he said, life is a thing of beauty, Gaber, and a joy for ever" (164).

Gaber steps upon the stage like a supernatural being to pronounce the denouement of the spectacle and departs to silent chords of malicious laughter. That is as far as one gets, impaled on orders en route to vagrancy.

3
Malone's Testament

In *Malone Dies*, the space of the entire performance is a small, bare room in which a bedridden old man writes with the stub of a pencil. The only light is from the window, a dirty grayish light, which falls on the bed set lengthwise against it. We do not overhear his thoughts as he writes. He proclaims as on a stage, the stage of the mind where the self is galvanized by the spectacle of a man who, in fighting to remain true to the ruins that he has made of his life, is also fighting for justice, perhaps. "Perhaps"—because both the reader and Malone are torn by two perspectives on Malone's situation. Is he one of the accursed, whose lingering death is a prefiguration of his damnation to come? Or is he a type of the heroic Prometheus, steadfast against complicity and harried into being his own destroyer?

Malone addresses us with his first words: "I shall soon be quite dead at last in spite of all" (179). He has a strong presentiment that his hour has come. "But in what does it differ from those that have abused me ever since I was born? No, that is the kind of bait I do not rise to any more" (179). He will not be carried by the connecting mucous of language to feeling anxious about his life. He smiles, "my need for prettiness is gone" (179)— that is, the grand narrative of Reward and Punishment.

He wishes to "die, quietly, without rushing things" (179). Evidently there is pressure in the background, the reproach of memory, the need to sum things up. To this impulse he replies, "I shall die tepid, without enthusiasm. I shall not watch myself die, that would spoil everything" (179). And sarcasm being insufficient to smother a persistent uneasiness, he attacks with

indignation. "There he is now, my old debtor", the image of the
Malone of the past, "Shall I then fall on his neck?" (180)—take
the profligate, the reprobate, the old whore-son, in my arms?
Or, in the terms of payment due, is the figure coming to meet
him Jesus? If the Exalted, then he should fall on his knees. But
the notion of the "old debtor" mocks such an idea. Life owes
Malone. "I shall not answer any more questions," he says. "I
shall tell myself stories, if I can" (180). Why? He literally
shrieks the answer: to feel himself repaid, to get some satisfaction at showing life for what it is. "Let me say before I go any
further that I forgive nobody. I wish them all an atrocious life
and then the fires and ice of hell and in the execrable genera-
tions to come an honoured name" (180). He refers to the edi-
fiers, models of propriety, the honoring of their names being the
greatest of infamies. The explosion blows to hell for the moment
the nagging feelings of self-disgust instilled in him by the "honoured."

Yes, he will tell stories, but he has no intention of being carried by them inadvertently into the muck of his past. Yet he
worries about when to give an inventory of his possessions,
what stories and when to tell them, as if whatever he did might
turn into an occasion for self-reflection. He turns snide: "All my
life long I have put off this reckoning, saying, Too soon, too soon.
Well it is still too soon. All my life long I have dreamt of the
moment when, edified at last, in so far as one can be before all is
lost, I might draw the line and make the tot. This moment
seems now at hand. I shall not lose my head on that account"
(181).

Here is Malone, the pin of conscience impaling him, standing
his ground, defying the notion of a comeuppance, as if his monstrously prolonged life were not atonement enough. Story time.
"The old fog calls" (182).

He lays out a program for the remaining brief interval of his
life, determined not to wriggle. The game afoot is suppression,
the nullification of a probing conscience. He describes his circumstances, but with an eye on surfaces, writing as playtime. To
play is to divert attention by dilating wittily. "I have lived in a
kind of coma. The loss of consciousness for me was never any
great loss" (183). Wisecracking, the discharge of anxiety: "The

truth is, if I did not feel myself dying, I could well believe myself dead, expiating my sins, or in one of heaven's mansions" (183). To play means transmuting anxiety into flourishes. What else is successful creation but a grand mastery of such flourishes? He must maintain his buoyancy, stay afloat, a kind of bobbing in the dissolving element of conscience.

He describes his room, his attendant whom he never sees, his long stick with a hook at the end. "Thanks to it I can control the furthest recesses of my abode. How great is my debt to sticks!" (185). He describes his enfeebled body, his degree of impotence, his posture in the bed. "Sometimes I miss not being able to crawl around any more. But I am not much given to nostalgia" (186). Whatever else he may be, he is a master of the punch line.

All at once, writhing from that merciless pin, he cries out in defiance: "I shall not speak of my sufferings" (186)—the smothering migraines of a probing conscience. "On others let it wreak its dying rage, and leave me in peace" (186). Rage at whom, the exemplary?—displace, extirpate guilt by hating his fictional others? A strong motive for storytelling. "Such would seem to be my present state" (186), which we might entitle, "The Spinning Top," or "Spinning Tot," or "Bub in the Nest Croaking."

Why are we flippant? It must be a momentary loss of nerve. We are played upon by the bowstring of the novel. Our doubts emerge. Whose justice? Do we smile and adhere to our Promethean hero? Or do we scorn him for spiritual suicide, for flouting the elevated "I," a longing for the divine?

The terrible repetition of resolution and failure is like one of the endless, circular punishments of Dante's *Inferno*. Never to say, "O great God, grant me grace to really look into myself, have mercy on me Father in God, who, with undeviating laws eternal, yet careth for the falling of the feather from the sparrow's wing." Beckett plays us like a musical instrument by presenting us with a man who expresses repugnance for the higher concerns of morality and is attracted to the indecencies of taste; at the same time Beckett tunes us to believe that there is no more radical act of spirit than in Malone's being himself, martyr of the great refusal.

Malone begins the story of the Saposcats, humdrum, banal people who have a simpleton for a son. Malone calls him Sapo, and chooses him for his hero because Sapo's mind is as empty as an abandoned hive—ergo, an instrument for play. But he breaks off with scarcely an introduction. "What tedium" (187), he exclaims, dropping the thread of his story, not out of boredom, but migraine. The exasperated cry—"What tedium"—becomes formulaic for that unremitting pressure to prostrate himself.

He hits a note of pathos in describing his body as an aged hunting dog that cannot respond to the master's whistle, and whose weak barking and wagging remind the master, "It is time I had him destroyed" (192). It is not self-pity; it is Malone, always the connoisseur of the nice effect.

Picking up again the thread of his story, he says, "Nothing is less like me than this patient, reasonable child. . . . Yes, now my mind is easy, I know the game is won" (193)—and immediately catches himself on the phrase "impending dawn" (194) for sunrise. The cliché, like a binding mucus, belies the idea of his being himself, whatever that may be; it erodes the very notion of his being in control. There follows a swift, seamless transition from a feeling of helpless vulnerability, and implicit "whose lines do I speak?" to his outbraving his fear of an unintelligible damnation in which every word is scripted and will repeat like the tunes in a hurdy-gurdy.

He could not play the game of living. Trying had been his disease. He had tried with a frenzy of earnestness and failed. A time came when he submitted to failing as to a pledge. He would fail at living, a scrupulous obstinacy not to try again. So long as he can make stories, he can hope to escape being fictionalized by his own conscience, translated into the grand narrative as an abomination.

At the very onset of his Sapo story an idea emerges, a plan that would enable him to die on his terms—a synchrony of deaths. "Then live, long enough to feel, behind my closed eyes, other eyes close. What an end" (195). Sapo's death and his, simultaneously. Pulling it off would somehow prove that he exists, that he is not pasteboard in an edifying tableau.

But he is like a pot coming to boil, his body's sufferings increasing the pressure for self-reflection and the volatility of his moods. The moment he begins to think, his feelings drive him almost to agony. His dying is a martyrdom not to lose self-possession.

He explodes into the story of the Lamberts in an effort to regain his self-possession after being taken off-guard by a mood of serenity, a strange, childlike mood dragging with it the ruins that he has made of his life. "I turn a little on my side, press my mouth against the pillow, and my nose, crush against the pillow my old hairs now no doubt as white as snow, pull the blanket over my head" (198). On his back like a baby, his head turned about like a bird's and pressed into the pillow, he sucks on the pillow and draws the blanket over him like a shroud. Conscious of new pain, he feels that he is dying, and feels strangely happy, accepting and serene.

It is a blissful moment of release, or reprieve. He senses it passing—"[f]or the wise thing now would be to let go, at this instant of happiness" (199)—and cannot prevent his slipping back into himself, jarring back into the space of his *agon*. "All I want now is to make a last effort to understand, to begin to understand, how such creatures are possible" (199). He lashes out at the lives of ordinary people. But in the mood into which he is sinking, there is no point accusing and nothing to explain. Only sadness, sadness at his life's ruins, at having accomplished only the refusal. "The last word is not yet said between me and—yes the last word is said" (199). In this fathomless mood of regret, he concedes that his grotesque life is God's judgment.

Malone propels himself into the story of the Lamberts, forgetting Sapo and his planned ending for the while, and promptly finds his stride in a soothing depiction of Big Lambert, in his prime at eighty-four, consumed by lust for slaughtering pigs and for brutalizing his young wife, his third or fourth. He describes Mrs. Lambert, her hideous life of chores, and filth, and abuse, stroking out the sentences in a monotone, cold-bloodedly, in vengeance against his own bad conscience. Big Lambert, hardly more than a maniac with his lust for killing and brutality; his wife, hardly more than a madwoman from dashing her head repeatedly against the wall; Edmund, the son, gaps between his teeth, a scarcely tethered beast; and daughter Lizzy, merely a vessel to be used.

Malone takes vicious delight in climbing the register of savagery. Scene:

> Alone with his daughter Lambert sat watching her. She was crouched before the range, in an attitude of dejection. He told her to eat and she began to eat the remains of the rabbit, out of the pot, with a spoon. . . . [S]uddenly Lambert saw his daughter at another place and otherwise engaged than in bringing the spoon up from the pot into her mouth and down from her mouth into the pot. . . . He said, To-morrow we'll kill Whitey, you can hold her if you like. But seeing her still so bad, and her cheeks wet with tears, he went towards her. (216)

Malone breaks off. This is not play; he feels no buoyancy. His smile is like a little rictus full of malice, but he goes on with his story, in bitterness, lingering on Mrs. Lambert and resonating through her, the memory of his own grotesque existence.

> One day I took counsel of an Israelite on the subject of conation. That must have been when I was still looking for someone to be faithful to me, and for me to be faithful to. Then I opened wide my eyes so that the candidates might admire their bottomless depths and the way they phosphoresced at all we left unspoken. (217)

There follows an ugly, tawdry picture of his first homosexual encounter, illuminating and precisely registering the tone of the opening line to the passage. "One day I took counsel . . . " meaning, I asked a homosexual I was conjoining with what has brought us together, what underlies the attraction? Nauseated by himself, he continues, notwithstanding, to be transfixed by memories. Speaking of Jackson,

> I could have put up with him as a friend, but unfortunately he found me disgusting, as did Johnson, Wilson, Nicholson and Watson, all whore-sons. I then tried . . . to lay hold of a kindred spirit among the inferior races, red, yellow, chocolate, and so on. And if the plague-stricken had been less difficult of access I would have intruded on them too, ogling, sidling, leering, ineffing and conating, my heart palpitating. (218)

It rings convincingly, that admixture like quicksand, of self-hatred and remorse. "What tedium," he cries, struggling for self-possession. What had happened to his program for the remaining time?—"[a]nd I thought I had it all thought out" (218)—promptly turning to speculation on where he is, on precisely what floor, where-am-I speculations, and then, am-I-alive-or-not speculations. Has he been making a lot of fuss for himself for nothing? "But my horse-sense tells me I have not yet quite ceased to gasp. And it summons in support of this view various considerations having to do for example with the little heap of my possessions" (219–20). All this is so fluid, the movement from an embittered, raging despair and self-disgust to a snide removal, from the anguish of self-reflection to this game playing. Am I alive? Careful. Where am I? What floor? Am I sure there is only one basement? How do I know that there is not something akin to the activity of a hive going on, babies being moved about, up-down, all around, for some mysterious reason, perhaps to prepare them for their ambulatory days. The tone shifts to a leisurely, almost languid contemplation on the character and quality of the light in his room. Always he seeks to pick his way into further discrimination. It is a talent, an art, that keeps him bobbing.

"Ah yes, I have my little pastimes" (222). But these depend on his pencil and exercise book. What happens if he loses his pencil? Why, a panicky defenselessness. The pencil means safety. It confers confidence, like a magic wand. With it in hand he does a majestic improvisation on his situation:

> [to] see us again as we are, namely to be removed grain by grain until the hand, wearied, begins to play, scooping us up and letting us trickle back into the same place, dreamily as the saying is. For I knew it would be so, even as I said, At last! And I must say that to me at least and for as long as I can remember the sensation is familiar of a blind and tired hand delving feebly in my particles and letting them trickle between its fingers. And sometimes, when all is quiet, I feel it plunged in me up to the elbow, but gentle, and as though sleeping. But soon it stirs, wakes, fondles, clutches, ransacks, ravages, avenging its failure to scatter me with one sweep. (224)

The tone tantalizes. His delight in his own metaphorical skill momentarily extinguishes distress. It might seem a metaphor of

Nature at work divesting us of life grain by grain, inevitably to ransack and scatter, except that the "hand" is not Nature's. It is blind, tired, wakes, seems—on becoming conscious of what it is sifting—to repel the grains of Malone's being with disgust. Most likely the metaphor is meant to imply the Redeemer's distaste for the work of harvesting the likes of Malone, which captures Malone's situation precisely—ever the prey of his conscience and not yet delivered into its abjection.

"[B]allsaching poppycock," he calls his "launching forth" "about life and death, if that is what it is all about, and I suppose it is" (225). He gives the finger to life and death, to his monstrously prolonged life, the thought crossing his mind that he never would have chosen life. Possibly he was unborn. "Yes, an old foetus, that's what I am now, hoar and impotent, mother is done for, I've rotted her, she'll drop me with the help of gangrene" (225). "[P]erhaps papa is at the party too, I'll land head-foremost mewling in the charnel-house" (225)—birth, no doubt. "[N]ot that I'll mewl, not worth it. All the stories I've told myself, clinging to the putrid mucus" (225), holding on to mother, never being born, "swelling, swelling" (225), inside the womb, no doubt, "saying, Got it at last, my legend" (225), report from the womb Malone's great refusal? In this playful, always perilous mood of self-possession, Malone, after great wanderings, returns to Sapo. It is to be the last lap, his holding out in a whirling vortex to bring off a synchrony of deaths.

Yet in this movement to closure, Malone performs at his most engaging—dazzling displays of heroism in the ebullience of the comedy. He literally goes to his death in a display of fireworks. What are stories but acts of heroism, anxiety turned into comedy, phrases mounted and ridden gallantly, Malone superior to his desperation, until stricken by new pain, or by something reflected in his story, a ringing false note in his gaiety, and he is caught by the whirlpool, his life flashes before him, a compressing, strangling anguish of memories. This is the rhythm. Despair is loss of nerve. A recoup is always imminent. Gaiety transfigures dread. The comedy reestablishes his steadfastness, the throwing of life back in God's face like a worthless gift. Malone edified is the Unnamable who resists being born from knowledge of life.

For the finale, Malone's neglected hero (become a hapless bum whom he renames Macmann) is installed in a lunatic asylum. There, on the crest of two inspired narratives (Hairy Mac and Sucky Molly, and picnicking with Lady Pedal), and interludes that just come short of rivaling them (concerning keeper Lemuel, and Malone's visitor), he brings off the planned ending.

His visitor, whom he connects with what feels like a violent blow on the head, emerges out of an "[i]ncandescent migraine" (274). A phantom of his terror, it never gets hold of him. Dressed in a black suit, armed with a black umbrella, a black hat folded against his stomach in an attitude of piety, it is a hallucination inspired probably by the figure of the predatory Moran. The "long, dismal, glabrous, floury face" (269) is that of a vampire starving for blood. The caked mud on his boots terrifies Malone.

When his visitor leaves, perhaps to escort somebody else to an open grave, Malone composes himself, making a list of questions to show his visitor when next he comes, speculating on the meaning of the visit, and, middle finger raised, springing off into shameless ribaldry. He turns his dread and the pressure for a reckoning, a spiritual inventory, into laughter, reinforcing for the edified the conviction that his life is an obscene joke whose punch line is shortly to evolve. Imagining all his judges lining up to give him a clout on the head like his visitor, Malone fancies his catching one:

> a little girl for example, and half strangle her, three quarters, until she promises to give me my stick, give me soup, empty my pots, kiss me, fondle me, smile to me, give me my hat, stay with me, follow the hearse weeping into her handkerchief, that would be nice. I am such a good man, at bottom, such a good man, how is it nobody ever noticed it? A little girl would be into my barrow, she would undress before me, sleep beside me, have nobody but me, I would jam the bed against the door to prevent her running away, but then she would throw herself out of the window, when they got to know she was with me they would bring soup for two, I would teach her love and loathing, she would never forget me, I would die delighted, she would close my eyes and put a plug in my arse-hole, as per instructions. Easy, Malone, take it easy, you old whore. (273)

So much for conscience.

The transports of Moll and Macmann, the stark particulars in the strivings of these old, deformed, impotent lovers summoning to their aid determination, mucus, and imagination, and succeeding in "a kind of sombre gratification" (260), carries Malone merrily along, until fear of dying without having worked out his plan obliges him to kill Moll and replace her with Lemuel. Malone deputizes him the deceased Moll's replacement, Macmann's keeper, a lunatic who stamps up and down for hours on end, flayed alive by memories, and upbraiding himself on the head with a hammer to quell his moral anguish. In the final scene of the novel, the excursion with Lady Pedal, Lemuel is the allegorical figure of Malone's despair who will transform into the good shepherd Death.

With his last gasps, Malone describes the retinue of lunatics, the five, counting Macmann, in Lemuel's keep, and their bountiful benefactor, "a huge, big, tall, fat woman. Artificial daisies with brilliant yellow disks gushed from her broad-brimmed straw hat" (284). The vomiting, gesticulating, and head-hammering of the ensemble on the way to the dinghy cannot daunt Lady Pedal's superb exuberance, which breaks forth in song, "*Oh the jolly spring*" (285).

Malone, too weak to dilate on the crossing to the island, rouses for the finale. Lady P is out of sight looking for a pleasant place to picnic. Lemuel kills the two escorting sailors with his hatchet. "The voice of Lady Pedal, calling. She appeared, joyous" (287). She faints, "holding in her hand a tiny sandwich" (287). Lemuel and the five in his keep launch out in the boat on a journey. The story sputters out in the broken gurgling voice of Malone in death.

Those final words in broken phrases state over and again that Lemuel will not use his hatchet any more, not strike anyone any more, never. He has become the good shepherd Lemuel. Malone dies in synchrony with Macmann. He dies "inutilizable," untranslated, true to his personal testament (*The Unnamable* 331).

4

Naming the Unnamable

1

The Unnamable, a confessional monologue like the other novels in the trilogy, consists entirely of the narrator's speculations about his "situation." Where the voice comes from must be inferred. Facts are impossible to ascertain. The strongest impression is of a voice emanating from a presence, a demiurge; it has been selected, its turn come round perhaps, to be born human, to undergo the passage. It refuses to cooperate. It does not want existence, and it/his courage enlists our admiration. He bears a faint resemblance, which he himself notes, to Prometheus. But where is he? Alone, in darkness, riveted in a fixed position. Is he in a pit? A dungeon? Does the space he inhabits have a shape? He speculates, and one speculation gives rise to another. He is being acted upon by a delegation of socializers—sadists—preparing and training him for existence. But how does he know what he knows about life? How is it he has what seem to be memories? Had he a prior existence? And who is he whom he calls himself? Can there be an "I," a self, that is not the construct of human shaping? This is desperate business, and there is nothing concrete, evidentiary, to go on. Can there be an "I," a me, a preexistent self prior to socialization, prelinguistic? If so, how can he get back to that self?

All his inquiries about who he is, and where, and why, and the conjectures and suppositions and stories they give rise to, constitute his force of arms, so to say, against the necessity of existing. It is what keeps him going and what keeps at bay the dreadful suspicion that he is speaking from dictation, that the personae of his stories are decoys tempting his acquiescence to the life process.

He combats despair with seemingly endless "perhapses," suppositions about his situation in which escape is possible. One of his favorite constructions, which he returns to for fortitude, postulates a master with an agenda opposite to that of the master's delegates, a persecutorial junta determined to give him existence. The master wants something from him, some perception of his situation, some word or words before releasing him; so he must go on in the hope of coming up with that something unbeknownst to him that will satisfy the master "before I can be let loose, alone, in the unthinkable unspeakable, where I have not ceased to be, where they will not let me be" (*The Unnamable* 335). His implacable aversion to being given a life generates parodies about life's triviality and awfulness, and gives meaning to his resistance. We are persuaded that his resistance is wise, which is one source of the novel's enthralling effect.

The narrator begins with the surmise that there is an "I" unshaped by life. But it is only surmise. In any case, he cannot reinhabit that time. Therefore, "It" would be more appropriate than "I." "It, say it, not knowing what" (291). True, he speaks, but about what, whom—him? But presuming he has a presence, an "I," how differentiate his being from the constructs foisted upon it by others and by himself? Is there a rock-bottom, authentic, naked, palpitating, conscious "I" with its own sound? What sound? How sound it? The very voicing of words, language, vastly distances him from this prelinguistic self, if it exists at all. He refuses to cooperate, he does not want existence; but does not the ceaseless monologue prove he already exists? And why has he been put in such a situation? He is angry; he feels he has been had. He speaks on and on to get at the nub of himself while speaking at the same time prevents him from getting at the nub. What is necessary to find the core self, which in any case living will extinguish? "Perhaps in the end I shall smother in a throng. Incessant comings and goings, the crush and bustle of a bargain sale" (292). He wonders if he is a final recrudescence of consciousness, a vanishing presence still responding to intimations of a core self. Wherever he is—and the question "where?"

generates continuous speculation—it is preferable to the losing of self in life's repulsive clownishness.

Some of his speculations float off undeveloped, to be jettisoned; yet, for the moment, they fuel his will to protest. His only fuel is speculation.

Perhaps the "I" he is in search of is the "he" condemned to the opaque void he inhabits and perhaps always inhabited. He thinks of Lucifer punished for protesting creation; but why, he wonders, does he emulate creation, making up stories, representing life, babbling ideas that are not his own? Can such knowledge be innate, or has it all "been rammed down my gullet" (298)? Fellow feeling, love, a moral sense—he snorts at these travesties. Despite his deep suspicion of his personae, he chooses to speculate that his creative drive expresses an obscure need to find and reveal his true self, a frenzy to speak in order to achieve silence—the invisible retreat; speaking, endless speaking, fictionalizing, creating, in the hope of hitting upon the magic word, the open door, to his core self; that through misdirection and lies he may chance upon the truth that will free him from his torment.

Torment, physical torment: "my body incapable of the smallest movement" (300–301). His eyes are incapable of closing, "but must remain forever fixed and staring on the narrow space before them. . . . They must be as red as live coals" (301). So he perseveres; he must go on in order to end. "[T]o end would be wonderful, no matter who I am, no matter where I am" (302).

Dread arises at the prospect of some ghastly recurrence, the process endlessly repeating itself, his refusal scripted. The question, what drives him and toward what, when he creates, that is, orders experience by speaking, cuts to the heart of his situation. Dread compels him to return to it repeatedly. What if he were being driven to speak "in obedience to the unintelligible terms of an incomprehensible damnation" (308)? His attention ought instead to be fixed on the "feeble murmur" of the essential self, barely audible because of the noise he was making. He speculates that it might "be better if [he] were simply to keep on saying babababa" than drone on with suppositions and stories which tempt him away from his essential self (308). For the "he" in the stories he tells, the persona-narrator, Mahood, speaks with his voice, with a voice woven into his, testifying for him, living in his stead, "preventing me from saying who I was, what I was" (309). Why does he do it, then? Out of compulsion? A new speculation emerges: "Yes, I have a pensum to discharge, before I can be free. . . . I was given a pensum, at birth perhaps, as a punishment for having been born perhaps, or for no particular reason, because they dislike me" (310). How did it come about, this inner need to speak, that is, to become complicit in his socialization, education, existence? Ah, the sadists molding him, Basil, the most hateful, had made him feel an inner need to expiate his recalcitrance. He creates Mahood, Basil internalized, in order to discharge the pensum and "obtain his [master's] forgiveness" (311). He makes up stories in order to please his master, who really intends to reward his resistance.

He has found a loophole through a fairy tale: forgiveness for not allowing himself to be stifled, for holding out. But what is it that his master wants to hear? "Let the man explain himself and have done with it. It's none of my business to ask him questions, even if I knew how to reach him. . . . assuming he exists and, existing, hears me" (313).

He provides other speculations: he posits a junta of masters differing in their opinions of what they want from him; and then wonders why they do not just wash their hands of him; and further speculates that it is all a lie, that he invented the whole "business of a labour to accomplish, before I can end, of words to say, a truth to recover . . . in the hope it would console me, help me to go on" (314). He contradicts each speculation and then contradicts the contradiction, on and on, running to stay in place.

But he is resilient. He tries the old pathways again, seeking new avenues of speculation, which is his only way of challenging futility. So, prodding at the motive of his creative drive, he speculates that his persona, Mahood, is a decoy, a lure, and a usurper cozening him into being a living human specimen. "Then they uncorked the champagne. One of us at last! Green with anguish! A real little terrestrial!" (316). Well, then, he decides mockingly, a story to tempt him toward conformity, a story to give satisfaction to his teachers, a story about the "me" they would have him admit to being.

"In a word I was returning to the fold" (317). In the new story, he, Mahood, the one-legged wanderer on crutches, arrives at what appears more like a concentration camp than a home: a "vast yard or campus, surrounded by high walls, its surface an amalgam of dirt and ashes" (317); the family house "windowless, but well furnished with loopholes" (317); all his kith and kin "[w]ith their eyes glued to the slits" (318) watching at night "with the help of a searchlight" (318). They spot him and cheer. And then they all die, "the whole ten or eleven of them, carried off by sausage-poisoning" (318).

The idea of ties, liability to pain, of being schooled, made delicately susceptible to suffering in a world licking its chops, a Schopenhauerian world, or better yet, Hitlerian, a world of catastrophe—"this circus where it is enough to breathe to qualify for asphyxiation"—goads the Unnamable into several different accounts of his homecoming (323). Was he repelled, turned back "by the noise of their agony, then by the smell of their corpses" and "wafts of decomposition" (321, 322)? No, he reasons, the truth more likely is that he did not turn aside and vomit, beating a retreat from the stench and groans. He entered the building.

> [A]nd there completed my rounds, stamping under foot the unrecognizable remains of my family, here a face, there a stomach, as the case might be, and sinking into them with the ends of my crutches, both coming and going. To say I did so with satisfaction would be stretching the truth. For my feeling was rather one of annoyance at having to flounder in such muck. (323)

The point of this extravaganza is to stick it to his teachers. "Do they consider me so plastered with their rubbish that I can never extricate myself, never make a gesture but their cast must come to life" (325)? But the more likely truth is that "[t]hey've blown me up with their voices, like a balloon," and that there is no escaping speaking "in the way they intend [him] to speak, that is to say about them, even with execration and disbelief" (325, 326).

He decides to tell another one of Mahood's stories. Why? "To heighten my disgust," he says, that is, disgust for them, his tormenters, or disgust at playing into their hands (326). But he also speculates, "Perhaps I'll find traces of myself" (325).

Mahood II is a strangely heroic version of the narrator's situation: an impish little fellow without arms and legs, housed in a deep glass jar, so very brave under the circumstances, his jar festooned with Chinese lanterns and the menu of the restaurant across the street. He hangs as an advertisement. In part it is a joke, an entertainment, an escape from self, and how the tale keeps him going, imagining this Mahood thinking away the day, earning an income, maintaining a relationship with the proprietress of the chophouse, who changes his straw once a week, a competent social unit bestowing his benison on the proprietress's family in the way of fertilizer for their kitchen garden during the growing season, nothing but a puckish grin on his face when his mouth had been visible, before having been throttled by a cement collar.

Inevitably the narrator's distrust and fear of his creative drive kills it. He returns to himself, his mood brittle and volatile. He is being sported with. His creative urge has been instilled in him by the enforcers, and serves their ends, not his. He must hold out against their influence, refusing life "until they have abandoned me as inutilizable" (331). Then the master will "give me quittance" (331). Or, the more desperate version of the fairy tale: it is only by pleasing his persecutors, that is, giving vent to his creative drive, and perhaps in portraying "how to succeed at last" in being human, that he may please his master. According to this theory, he must lose himself, "behave as if he were not," by creating fictional self-representations, thereby taking on existence, and believe in the lie, before being allowed to go silent (334). He must deny his intrinsic self with conviction in order to receive his master's praise. Here, the creative urge is an angling for mercy. "The essential is to go on squirming forever at the end of the line" (338).

A sudden playful mood leads him back to Mahood II. He enters his persona, recalling times before the collar had stifled him. A fatalistic tone slips in: if only he could die. But how does he know that he himself is an autonomous being, alive? Immediately the narrator expresses his predicament as Mahood II, the bottle dweller, who is suddenly aware that nobody takes notice of him, not even those who stop to study the menu attached to his jar. How could this be? "The flies vouch for me, if you like, but how far? Would they not settle with equal appetite on a lump of cowshit?" (341).

The game afoot is how to prove he exists. The narrator's loop-hole is his fairy tale—pleasing his master, proving to be one of the "chosen shits" of "a sporting God" (338). His existence is based on his wavering faith in the existence of a master who loves him. As for the little rascal in the jar, he finds proof of his substantiality in the proprietress's attention to him. "Would she rid me of my paltry excrements every Sunday, make me a nest at the approach of winter, protect me from the snow, change my sawdust, rub salt into my scalp, I hope I'm not forgetting anything, if I were not there?" (343). Why, she must love him!

The novel's form—of constant contradiction, modification, and counter speculation, or more precisely, of hopeful constructions negated in reiterated variations—creates the illusion of perpetual motion, a going round and round in endlessly circling interpretations of the narrator's situation. Three affirmative constructions give rise to numerous negations:

1. The Unnamable narrator speaks in order to catch a trace of his essential self, his intrinsic "I" trying to emerge, but the characters he has created, his various personae, the Murphys, Molloys, Malones, and Mahoods, reveal to him nothing about himself, and he continues to doubt that he has an independent existence.

2. He speaks to put an end to things, to come upon a formula, a phrase, that will free him from the necessity to speak. But his stories—representations of himself "in the midst of men, the light of day"—are told under compulsion, part of his socialization (297). He is a mere puppet speaking from dictation whose existence is the enactment of an unintelligible damnation. He is trapped in a circuit, endlessly repeating himself, damned like the Sybil, condemned in a jar to an undying existence.

3. He speaks either to prove himself intractable and "inutilizable" or to display obedience to his socializers—losing himself in his personae, adapting to life, showing conviction—in either case in order to please his master and receive quittance. But the master remains distant, his purpose hidden, his torturers adept.

The fairy tale of a loophole, a spur to his ongoing monologue, is repeatedly exploded by two additional powerful negations: he speaks merely to console himself; he suffers merely to amuse his torturers.

Worm, a shadowy persona little more than a name, emerges as an occasion for describing the sadism of the socializers, the life-shapers. In some accounts, Worm is the embryo of the speaker:

> There he is now with breath in his nostrils, it only remains for him to suffocate. . . . A head has grown out of his ear, the better to enrage him. . . . It's a transformer in which sound is turned, without the help of reason, to rage and terror. . . . The rascal, he's getting humanized, he's going to lose if he doesn't watch out, if he doesn't take care, and with what could he take care, with what could he form the faintest conception of the condition they are decoying him into, with their ears, their eyes, their tears and a brainpan where anything may happen. (355–56, 360)

Worm's continuous persecution (birthing) elicits this and other anti-creation stories.

"The dirty pack of fake maniacs" (368) are expertly trained in what they do, till Worm is violated, had, sufficiently throttled: "[t]hen the blaze, the capture and the paean" (366). Then "diapers bepissed and the first long trousers" (378). But they won't catch the narrator.

The pace quickens, injecting a note of panic into the breathless protest. But safe in the labyrinth of speculation, he can still joke about the awfulness of life, and even parody his own aversion for it. The human specimen: "sight failing, chronic gripes, light diet, shit well tolerated, hearing failing, heart irregular, sweet-tempered, smell failing, heavy sleeper, no erections, would you like some more . . . yes, I was right, no doubt about it this time, it's you all over" (377).

Abjuration: "[S]ome people are lucky, born of a wet dream and dead before morning" (379–80).

But suddenly, the climax: a disabling and mortal acknowledgment is made, it would seem, admitting the futility of his protest. It could well serve as the culmination of the spectacle, signifying capitulation, if it did not occur some twenty-five pages from the end—if *The Unnamable* ended in defeat:

> [N]o need of a mouth, the words are everywhere, inside me, outside me . . . impossible to stop them, impossible to stop, I'm in

words, made of words, others' words, what others, the place too, the air, the walls, the floor, the ceiling, all words, the whole world is here with me, I'm the air, the walls, the walled-in one, everything yields, opens, ebbs, flows, like flakes, I'm all these flakes, meeting, mingling, falling asunder, wherever I go I find me, leave me, go towards me, come from me, nothing ever but me, a particle of me, retrieved, lost, gone astray, I'm all these words, all these strangers, this dust of words . . . and nothing else, yes, something else, that I'm something quite different, a quite different thing, a wordless thing in an empty place, a hard shut dry cold black place, where nothing stirs, nothing speaks, and that I listen, and that I seek, like a caged beast born of caged beasts born of caged beasts born of caged beasts born in a cage and dead in a cage, born and then dead, born in a cage and then dead in a cage, in a word like a beast, in one of their words, like such a beast, and that I seek, like such a beast, with my little strength, such a beast. (386–87)

Since he has no identity, if he speaks, it must be ventriloquism. If he can be said to have an identity, it is trapped in an inescapable circuit. And his hope of an end to his torment? Of course, the hope is fiction, too. There is no escaping existence.

A mind in search of a way out of its own circularity becomes frantic. Is the speaker "I," or do I speak from dictation? How do I know what I know? Can life be understood only from words? Why cannot this voice go silent? What can be said of the real silence? Where am I? "Enormous prison, like a hundred thousand cathedrals . . . and in it, somewhere, perhaps, riveted, tiny, the prisoner . . . it will be unending . . . wait somewhere else, for your turn to go again . . . it's a circuit, a long circuit . . . it's a lie . . . all lies" (409–11).

On and on goes the mind, accelerating, touching all the nodal points. From where did he get his stories? "[I]t's such an old habit, I do it without heeding" (413). Or, they are expressions of his fortitude to go on. Or, the life-shapers have taught him to internalize their lessons. Or, they are born out of a need to find traces of himself, the time that exists before the voice. "I'm waiting for me there." Or, "all words, there's nothing else" (414). And on and on.

2

The narrative consists of the reiterated variations of these speculations and counterspeculations, while within the work nothing progresses (unless it be a breathlessness and tone of urgency and desperation). Perhaps the book is a portrayal of how a mind copes with inevitability. The inevitability is death, inverted in the novel so that life becomes inevitable, while the labor of denial, the pathetic strategies to which one clings for solace, remain the same. The inversion, in which life takes on the repugnance usually reserved for death, broadens the satire on human existence. The novel, then, may seem to explore and give fullness to Camus's statement that the only question worth answering is whether or not to commit suicide. Is the Unnamable heroic, Promethean, the indomitable human spirit? Or does he represent the abjectness, the mean grubbiness, of the desire to live?

The portrayal needs to be a long piece because the reader must be made to endure this emotional state in time. The only dimension is time. There is no progression and no three-dimensional world. It all exists in a point. Could the book be a kind of formal design, a structure of prisms and refractions? One struggles to say what the novel suggests as an abstract composition.

In a "manifesto" on art, "Three Dialogues,"[6] which Beckett wrote in December 1949 when struggling with the final part of The Unnamable, he says that the true artist must turn away from "the plane of the feasible" in disgust, "weary of its puny exploits, weary of pretending to be able, of being able, of doing a little better the same old thing, of going a little further along a dreary road" (Disjecta 139). The only stance, he goes on to say, is "that there is nothing to express, nothing with which to express, nothing from which to express, no power to express, no desire to express, together with the obligation to express" (139). He dismisses the idea that he is calling for a minimalist art, stripped, abstract, expressive of the void, or inner emptiness. No, Beckett says: the artist must turn away from anything and everything "doomed to become occasion" for expression, including his predicament, which "is expressive of the impossibility to express"

(144, 143). "Art loves leaps" ("L'art adore les sauts," *Disjecta* 128),
he says, and notes in his letter to Axel Kaun, "[o]r is literature
alone to remain behind in the old lazy ways that have been
so long ago abandonded by music and painting. . . . An assault
against words in the name of beauty" (*Disjecta* 172, 173).

The main points of Beckett's aesthetic are these: Objective
unity is an illusion. Efforts to create coherent artistic form are
deadening falsifications. The essence of the object is resistance
to representation. The artist moreover is torn by a need to disparage his desire for order and structure and to disrupt it altogether. Art can only represent the instability of the subject and
the indeterminacy of the object. A new art form is needed, one
which of necessity must always be a failure both as objective
representation and as subjective expression. The artist either
strives for the new or is an antiquarian.

Perhaps *The Unnamable* can be discussed only as a series of
formal manipulations. Perhaps its effect is like that of a Rorschach blot, "unintentionally provocative; not a created object
but a creative one, or better still, no object at all but a concatenation of possibilities, limited by nothing but the mind's capacity
to endow shape with meaning."[7] Perhaps it is the shape of the
unheard hysteria that is the mental landscape of *Waiting for
Godot*. Beckett wrote the play as a "relaxation" before embark-
ing on *The Unnamable*. Perhaps the novel is the abstract music
of a frenzied collapsing of that small, private stock of ideas, the
permutations of which always protected one from an engulfing
sense of nothingness.

Within the broad critique of the human condition, *The Unnamable* expresses the artist's predicament, existing and drown-
ing in an uncertain and fluid world, striving without the means
for meaning. Beckett also searches for the source of artistic creation. Whomever the man is who is doing the talking, says Maurice Blanchot in his 1959 essay "Where Now? Who Now?," it is
not Beckett, "but the necessity that has displaced him," making
"him a nameless being," "masked . . . by a porous and agonizing
'I'" at "the empty, actuated site where the summons of the work
reverberates." What is enacted, Blanchot suggests, is "the funda-
mental exaction of the work" experienced at the search for its
point of departure. It cannot be authored in the sense of man-

aged, controlled, a product of the familiar, "the commodity of an available reality." The searching must be done stripped of most attributes of the world and involves a falling "out of the world," a "hovering between being and nothingness," where the self dissolves into its new creation. So the novel is an enactment of the process by which the author makes himself available as mediator to the unspoken.[8]

Andrew K. Kennedy adds "that what is being projected here is the writer's consciousness caught in a verbal no-man's land. . . . [a]t an imagined mid-point, somewhere between the discarded and not yet created personae."[9] Knowledge of the world is continuously being inflicted upon the speaking "I" by an external agency, deputies of some higher authority that would control, dictate the new genesis, interfering with the quasimagical incantation that will allow the artist to be silent, dissolving into his character.

> [Y]ou must say words, as long as there are any, until they find me, until they say me, strange pain, strange sin, you must go on, perhaps it's done already, perhaps they have said me already, perhaps they have carried me to the threshold of my story, before the door that opens on my story, that would surprise me, if it opens, it will be I, it will be the silence, where I am, I don't know, I'll never know, in the silence you don't know, you must go on, I can't go on, I'll go on. (*The Unnamable* 414)

In Anthony Uhlmann's philosophical study of Beckett's trilogy (1999), the Unnamable's resistance against the it/they attempting to absorb him is "one of extraordinary power."[10] At issue is his identity. But how prevail in his struggle to preserve it—how escape the labyrinth of language that is not his, and that in no way constitutes him? Uhlmann suggests that the Unnamable's desperate struggle exemplifies a striving for justice.

He develops his discussion in counterpoint with works of philosophy by Emmanuel Levinas and Jacques Derrida, underscoring the resonances, the philosophical ways of thinking, that shed light on the novel.[11] Beckett inverts Levinas for whom language is a link between the ego and others and is primarily aligned with justice. Injustice arises from the efforts of the ego to reappropriate the other into its totality. In *The Unnamable*, the other moves to appropriate the "I," or ego, "by plying it with its language and hauling it into the light of its day."[12] So, in Beckett, language is aligned with injustice, and the Unnamable is in the impossible situation of being enveloped in a closed system of injustice and violence, and striving for freedom.

What constitutes striving? Derrida suggests, says Uhlmann, ethical awareness, that is, responsibility for the hospitality of the world the newly born enter, and for keeping the lessons of history alive. It is a struggle against immurement in "the (fixed) presence of the present," which Derrida suggests is the worst form of injustice.[13] Derrida's phrase is close to the Russian *poshlost*, living a life without consequences or contexts. In Uhlmann's view, the Unnamable's resistance "is resistance to [Derrida's] entire discourse of self-presence,"[14] a dynamic picture of ethical striving for the impossibility of justice to which the alternative is spiritual death.

It seems possible that Beckett's Unnamable narrator merged in his mind with the idea of the Jew survivor of the Holocaust, giving him a powerful analogy for exploring the plight of the artist and a powerful image of ethical striving post-Holocaust. There are striking correspondences throughout the narrative: in the laments, which evoke concentration camps, annihilation camps; in the narrator's torments and fate, laced with the imagery of pits, fires, furnaces, ashes, and the implements of torture, and in the sadistic adeptness of his persecutors. The suggestive material is extensive and was likely drawn from Beckett's familiarity with and closeness to the German atrocities. Beckett spent the years 1942 to 1945 in Roussillon, a village in the southwest of Vichy France, living among Jews from all over Europe who had fled there and who were trying to survive the war. Initially, he was mistaken for a Jew. His biographer, James Knowlson, believes Beckett saw film footage in 1947 about the liberation of Belsen, Dachau, and Auschwitz, and that in the same year he read two remarkable memoirs describing life in Mauthausen.[15] The idea of the Jew behind the Unnamable is sustained by the narrator's "anonymity," "loss of self," "loss of all sovereignty," "utter uprootedness," "radical alienation" (terms from Blanchot's *The Writing of the Disaster*).[16] He, too, has been worn down past the nub to the point where all values have been exterminated, surviving in nihilistic desolation, where all objective order has been given up. He, too, is waiting, "awaiting a misfortune which is not still to come, but which has always already come upon [him]," a knowledge that impoverishes all experience (Blanchot, *Disaster* 18, 21).

Both the Unnamable narrator and the Jew survivor of the death camps have the double consciousness of different kinds of knowledge, which interact and intersect continuously. The distinction, in Blanchot's terms, is between "knowledge of the disaster," the reflection of a person in the secure present, a value-oriented and judgment-based remembering that seeks to reassure, to mediate, and to skirt the subversive experience of the devastation; and "knowledge as disaster," the unmediated experience of the devastation, which assaults the very integrity of the self. The Unnamable narrator exists at the site of anguished experience where the disaster is taking place. But for the survivor, the disaster is present as an absence. It is the "un-story" (Blanchot's term) in the Mahood stories (28).

Surviving in the normal world means in Blanchot's words:

> you are dead already, in an immemorial past, of a death which was not yours, which you have thus neither known nor lived, but under the threat of which you believe you are called upon to live; you await it henceforth in the future, constructing a future to make it possible at last—possible as something that will take place and will belong to the realm of experience. (65)

Through the lens of Blanchot, in *The Unnamable*, the "pensum," the need to go on, to exist, to create a self adapted for life in the normal world, expresses an inner need to pay off a debt for not having died. Death is the "un-story" in the Mahood stories, death invading the space of survival, "absence in its vivacity," "[making] the real impossible and desire undesirable" (Blanchot, *Disaster* 51, 66)—relentlessly reducing the personae, stripping away their humanity in a progression from one-legged Mahood I to limbless Mahood II to shadowy Worm. Both Mahoods are dying deaths they have not lived or known.

The Unnamable narrator depends on and suspects his personae, needing to enact his death through them, but distrusting their commerce with life. The voices glide into one another, merge, and become double voiced. Mahood I suggests that some human bonds are inviolable while simultaneously mocking such an idea. Mahood II maintains a measure of humanity while simultaneously excluding himself from the cosmic order, giving a terrible poignancy to his ludicrous parody of imposing a meaningful sequence on the details of his life.

The Unnamable character, in the hell of deep memory, keeps himself going by creating personae through whom he enacts his death, a totally paradoxical killing of the self by the self in order to keep the self alive. Death is due; it is an atonement. Wrapping his death in the mythology of life is a part of the atonement; for the exposing of lies, the mocking of life, the parody, condemns existence and maintains the austere imaginative space within which the Unnamable atones for continuing an existence in which his death is due.

There is no closure. The demand for closure would be a demand for moral meaning. Similarly, the staples of fiction—plot, description, symbol, dialogue, scene, a sense of character—imply consequence and are discarded. There are no lessons, there is no consoling future. Life is disaster.

Hence, the Unnamable narrator speaks from "the absolute passiveness of total abjection" (Blanchot, *Disaster* 15). Between life and death, that is where he is, crushed, a destroyed man—a mussulman (in the concentration camps, one who gives up). The voice is the interior life of the mussulman, who is neither living nor dead, refusing, resisting both life and death.

His consciousness is at a remove from the reality of the camp. His former life seems a dream; he does not believe in it, or that the he in it, if it is a memory, is he. He cannot be sure he has a self, an "I," apart from the master. He longs for a former time, but a time out of the world, a time in which he existed in the peace and silence of a restful mind. Clinging to that keeps him going, though the end must be a given, his fate in the hands of the master.

His eyes, mental eyes, are never shut; but there is no light in them. He would not see the world they would wrest him into. The voice of his thought is continuous, a soundless, incessant noise. It is his universe's element, his world's oxygen, a realm between nothingness, oblivion, and the master's domain, where his agents, whom he can no longer see or hear, would inflict upon him the horror of life.

Why then not simply oblivion? Why does he lie to himself, tease himself about escape, "quittance," from this realm between nothingness and horror to another "unthinkable unspeakable" existence? He cannot answer this question. He dreads and evades it, and spins round and round it. He knows that his ceaseless thinking is madness, yet believes that his madness is a kind of vigilance and refusal. Blanchot says that a mute protest rises out of the crushed victim's refusal to be blamed for the crimes of his persecutors, and also out of his tormented need to be held accountable, to "answer for the impossibility of being responsible." His continued existence is a bond of "friendship for that which has passed leaving no trace" (*Disaster* 25, 27).

So he protests, keeping that other world at a remove, enclosed within his thoughts, railing at his persecutors and resisting his own oblivion. He can even laugh, not at the life of the camp, known, felt, seen suggestively through the glaze of his retraction, sometimes almost starkly seen, as in, "the distant gleams of pity's fires biding their hour to promote us to ashes" (*The Unnamable* 306). His laughter is turned rather on the former world, the once-normal world, serving to buoy him like a life preserver leaking air: the cynical cracks about human nature, black retellings of the story of creation, wisecracks about the overrated human emotions, grotesqueries concerning the ties that bind, mad cacklings about the average human specimen, and on and on, though he may be merely a rat treading water in a tall pail, encouraged, wagered on, a sporting event, kept going by the dumb, elementary force of life.

Perhaps his Mahood tales arise on the insistent tide of this force, stories about a former life in a former world, but sardonically afflicted by his knowledge of the world as it is. He would laugh if the question of his continuing were not desperate, and if laughter, the feeling of freedom in its burst and expansiveness, did not instantly petrify under the scrutiny of the master grasping him by the chin with a hand like a cement collar.

What did the master want of him—oblivion? Life? If they were the only alternatives, if the other, the possibility of "quittance," of being "let loose, alone, in the unthinkable unspeakable," was a lie, he could not goad himself to take another step (*The Unnamable* 335). But, "impossible to find out, that's where you're buggered," and "[t]he best is not to decide anything, in this connexion, in advance. . . . Time will tell," and so forth, and so on, and inevitably "slipping, though not yet at the last extremity, towards the resorts of fable" (*The Unnamable* 412, 292, 308).

In this way he keeps at bay the absurdity of his hope of quittance. He blows bubbles and then bursts them, taking a modicum of strength from his jaunty moods, before blowing them again, and bursting them again, when with bitter jocularity he tells it as it is, sucking it up, breasting forward: "You've been sufficiently assassinated, sufficiently suicided, to be able now to stand on your own feet, like a big boy," and "They can't do everything. They have put you on the right road, led you by the hand to the very brink of the precipice, now it's up to you, with an unassisted last step, to show them your gratitude" though the whole production is nothing more than a moribund's dreadful subterranean activity (*The Unnamable* 333).

There are three principal aspects of the Unnamable. The condemned Jew merges into the author's muse disaffiliating itself from the creative act, and also into the Son of God refusing a Second Coming. Beckett's voice shifts among these facets, all of them repelled by the world—that of the Jew suspended between life and death, of the artist in mortal conflict with his creativity, and of the Son punished for refusing to serve a world that is beyond redemption.[17]

This, then, is the Unnamable: the foregrounded story of the three-in-one as answer to the Three-in-One God, attesting to the impossibility of bearing responsibility, the uselessness of bearing witness, the meaninglessness of self-sacrifice, and the nobility of hoping for nothing—hope creating out of its own wreck an heroic story of his situation. A mind in darkness contrives to survive under unspeakable torture—in a black void with nothing but consciousness, no limbs, no lips, attentive to the sound of his own thoughts though uncertain whose thoughts, the crux of the torture being doubt of his own existence—and from nothing creating himself, adversaries, the meaning of his struggle against Omnipotence, the great Punisher; inventing Molloy and Moran as deadbeat Christ and apostle, and Malone as an unaccepting Job, sufferers and heroes of his pain. He invents obscurities, shifts, games with language and with philosophical allusions—resting the mind for the elaborate framework and dramatics of the saga, who he is, where he is, why he is where he is, and what next? To refuse to pray or to howl to be put out of his misery are gestures of defiance; best of all, impotent as he is against Omnipotence, he goes on embellishing, searching, weaving the colossal fabric that is the story of his persecutions. The punishers cannot make him choose to live in the world of their creation. The text is a compendium of "their" methods and his manner of eluding them, his rallies and panics, the relentlessness and facetiae of a mind on high alert as in paranoid schizophrenia. He is the new figure of epic grandeur for the age of Kafka and the death camps.

Torture and Art:
Chapters 5–8

Prelude to Torture and Art

The idea of a torture chamber as the subject of Samuel Beckett's *Imagination Dead Imagine* (a work of a thousand words written first in French and then in English in 1965) is integral to a linkage I see between *Texts for Nothing* (1951), *Endgame* (1956), *How It Is* (1961), and *The Lost Ones* (1970). The stance and tone of the monologue may only become clear on the second reading. It is an exhibit unveiled by a connoisseur of torture relishing a little invention of his imagination. Guilefully he draws the reader in: "No trace anywhere of life, you say, pah, no difficulty there, imagination not dead yet, yes, dead, good, imagination dead imagine."[1] But whether or not it is possible to imagine imagination dead, the narrator has other aims. Already conceived in that "all white" is a white rotunda. "No way in, go in, measure" (182). We follow. The directive, "measure," makes clear that he knows what he is up to, and is not improvising as he goes along.

"Diameter three feet, three feet from ground to summit of the vault" (182), just room for the bodies of a man and woman lying back to back, head to arse, knees bent in fetal position, each pair of hands identically clasping knee and elbow—the two, "partner[s]" (184). They are breathing. They are motionless "but for the left eyes which at incalculable intervals suddenly open wide and gaze in unblinking exposure" (184). They are conscious of each other, having once for ten seconds caught sight of one another out of a corner of an eye.

The details of their story are not imagined. Their story is the torture chamber, the contrivance of a rotunda, where perhaps they had sat reading of Sir Lancelot and Guinevere's first kiss with sweating palms. The sadism is Dantesque in this private exhibition set up by a rather stagy villain very much the connoisseur of violent sensations, rubbing his hands with anticipation as he invites us to take a seat. Possibly we're participating in the maniacal torture by consenting to imagine a sin that warrants it; but here there is no why, any more than there is in Kafka's officer's torture of his victims in "In the Penal Colony."

Their bodies are sweating. In the whiteness it is hot. But then it turns gray and is colder until the freezing point when black is reached. Intervals between white and black, hot and cold, most often occur in an even cadence of twenty seconds. Less often there are pauses, resumptions, reversals of irregular length during the "feverish greys" when "all vibrates, ground, wall, vault, bodies" (183)—irregular spasms between an otherwise even alternation from extreme to extreme—"world still proof against enduring tumult," "world" being the calmative provided by the creator of the apparatus, the *conoscente* who moderates pain with periods of respite "and never twice the same storm" (184).

The bodies show no signs of decay. Whether or not the faces reveal torment is unclear. Both "seem to want nothing essential" (184) and yet "[i]t is clear however, from a thousand little signs too long to imagine, that they are not sleeping" (185). In other words, he must imagine them healthy enough to suffer to the maximum. This penchant for prolonging the pleasure of torturing is reinforced by the *conoscente*'s, "Only murmur ah, no more, in this silence, and at the same instant for the eye of prey the infinitesimal shudder instantaneously suppressed" (185). He is ravening at the feast and takes a special pleasure in controlling his delight in order to make it last.

"Leave them there, sweating and icy, there is better elsewhere" (185)—better prey, better prospects of torture, too enticing for the speaker to shut the eye of imagination or to imagine it dead. But then in fact he closes his eye, imagines that he has lost the rotunda and will never find out "if they still lie still in the stress of that storm, or of a worse storm, or in the black dark for good, or the great whiteness unchanging, and if not what they are doing" (185). He feels sated for the moment on the victims of his little invention, which he will return to, reentering the rotunda, should he imagine there is more to be wrung from them.

A key to the advance from the torment of ambivalence in *Texts for Nothing* to the acceptance of human cruelty in *How It Is* and to the controlled experiment of cruelty and stupidity in *The Lost Ones* is the discovery of the importance of torture to the imagination. *Endgame* can be seen as a step in the direction of the discovery revealed so baldly in *Imagination Dead Imagine*—imagination personified and confined to a rotunda where it survives on torture.

5

To Kafka with love or
Texts for Nothing

Texts for Nothing (written in French in 1951, translated into English by the author in 1966) follows the trilogy by one year. Beckett said of the work that it "was an attempt to get out of the attitude of disintegration, but it failed,"[2] a remark that may have a lot to do with the work being misunderstood and neglected. By and large commentators find *Texts* derivative, a coda to *The Unnamable*, and less than brilliant or compelling. They think of the individual texts as philosophical investigations, and read them, I feel, as if tone deaf. According to Knowlson and Pilling (1980), the texts are failed strategies to settle the question of whether or not the narrator exists. They see no principle of organization, and find many of the texts vacuous, without a center, diffuse, unadventurous, confused and confusing. Most critics slight the work.

More to my taste, Susan D. Brienza (1987) describes *Texts* as "the only story within a style that embodies its own futility."[3] Circular, repetitive, anxious, sometimes frenzied, ultimately dying out, the narrator's quest for embodiment, the quest of the "I" in pursuit of himself, ends in disembodied resignation to silence. Its diagram, Brienza says, is "thirteen small overlapping circles within one large zero."[4] For Brienza, style is the subject, the devices and elements of a style that envelops the narrator and makes funny and futile his attempts to locate himself, to know if he exists, to know anything.

Elliot Krieger (1977) describes, one might say, the effect on the reader of these stylistic devices. He imagines that the narrative "I" is the text itself and that each text prevents any attempt to inject plot and character. Where the rudiments of story lines exist, they are intentionally blocked from developing into a full narration. The chief point of this for Krieger is the contemplation of the reading of narration. "[W]e are kept conscious that the real creation occurs in our heads."[5] This may be all too true—that my reading of *Texts* is more a creation of my mind's participation than a literal understanding of the ink on the page.

Circular and repetitive but nevertheless displaying variety, the medley of thirteen plays on the themes that life is impossible and life in the imagination is unbearable. They seem like reveries or dreams, lacking a regulative intention. Writing in that trance-induced state, at once in the dark cellar and at his desk, Beckett conveys the way dreams move and voices the dream's hypnotic tone. *Texts* seem "like messages from another world," like an "obscure underground thinking, a graphology of the night mind." Beckett may have regarded *Texts* as creative probings, leaping-off points in the search for other doorways out of the material of the trilogy. As such, it is a "mimetic-expressive mirror" of his imagination at work.[6] Perhaps the mistake has been to see *Texts* as philosophical sketches rather than a cycle of prose poems about inspiration, paralysis, and the creative process that Kafka more than any other writer embodies.

In *Text 1* the narrator can still take refuge in the imagination. "Suddenly, no, at last, long last, I couldn't any more, I couldn't go on" (75)—go on living among the respectable, though going on deceiving, flattering himself about the life of the imagination is the dominant theme of the medley.[7] "Someone said, You can't stay here" (75). He evokes Molloy in describing the place: "Quag, heath up to the knees, faint sheep-tracks, troughs scooped deep by the rains. It was far down in one of these I was lying" (75). What possessed him to come? He stands outside himself remarking in the third person. Voices of the conventional world berate him to go home, sickened by the derelict figure flat on its face in the mud. The distinction between here on the heights and there in the valley is reminiscent of Hardy's "Wessex Heights."

"What possessed you to come?" insist the voices of the respectable (75). He shrugs. Up there, "noise" of the "sopping peat," "gulfs of quiet," "wind drowns, my life and its old jingles" (77). Under compulsion is his answer, dragged to the heights by his feet. "Eye ravening patient in the haggard vulture face, perhaps it's carrion time" (77). An allusion to Prometheus, here crucified by society. "I'm up there and I'm down here, under my gaze," being tortured and therefore derelict, "foundered, eyes closed, ear cupped against the sucking peat" (77).

Soon night falls and he can't go down in any case. Soon with night the mist clears and he can travel on. Contradictions, the "mingl[ing]" of "times and tenses" (78), the balking of continuity with non sequiturs, are stylistic devices abstracting the clear outlines and foregrounding them. He is what he is because it is too punishing to be other than what he is, and because "the big words" (78) are not big to him—home, mother, father, God, love; no lure in them for him. He is at home in his projections, like the tramps, Molloy and Macmann, mortal images of his disembodied voice, his travelers. They mutter, "the same old mutterings, the same old stories, the same old questions and answers" (78). Whose? Theirs, his, they are one and the same, he and his invariable projections, "always muttering, to lull me and keep me company, and all ears always, all ears for the old stories" (78).

He recalls his father telling him stories, and how he would relive those recollections in stories of his own, he become his father and himself, the man enchanting and the boy avidly listening, he holding himself in his arms in the light of the old family lamp, "tired out with so much talking, so much listening, so much toil and play" (79). In this text he is at peace with himself through being at odds with the world.

Text 2 provides a sharp contradiction: he cannot make the effort to live through his imagination. The narrator speaks divorced from his projections, his derelict outsiders, in some elsewhere removed from the world. Here he is, he says to himself, "under a different glass" (81), a specimen. He might invest himself in telling a story, "See the cliffs again, be again between the cliffs and the sea, reeling shrinking with your hands over your ears, headlong, innocent, suspect, noxious" (81). He is both attracted and repelled by the urge to tell a story.

He scans for potential characters. "See Mother Calvet again, creaming off the garbage before the nightmen come. She must still be there. With her dog and her skeletal baby buggy" (81). The thought of a morally instructive story rich with beauty and poetry disgusts him. "If only it could be wiped from knowledge" because the one collective lie about life fed to the living sustains the living like an anesthesia (82).

As for him, wherever he is, he has lost the will to go on. "[T]he subject dies before it comes to the verb, words are stopping too" (82). He cannot make the effort to live through his imagination. He cannot do it, endure it, endure where he is and what he is. Conscious of dying, revolted by himself, wanting to end, he notwithstanding improvises with memories, the old habit of working things up for a story, in order to keep living.

A church sexton ringing the Sunday service bells, Mr. Joly, with a stump for one of his legs, enters his mind. But he can't go on. The idea of churchgoers repels him. He tries again and momentarily loses himself in mentally sketching landscapes. As for inventing characters, an encounter, a story, "Bang! No" (84). He tries one more most tentative sketch and drops it. "There, it's done, it ends there, I end there" (84). Yet he cannot give the blank no to being's yes.

In *Text 3* he mocks the persistence of his creative drive, resuming facetiously, "there's going to be a story" (85), as if he were being led by the nose.

> Here, depart from here and go elsewhere. . . . there must be a body . . . I'll say I'm a body, stirring back and forth, up and down, as required. . . . all that is needed to live again . . . I'll say it's me, I'll get standing, I'll stop thinking, I'll be too busy, getting standing, staying standing, stirring about, holding out. (85)

And let the scene be springtime. "[T]hat puts the jizz in you" (85).

He will project himself into a character; he will will it. Why? He won't inquire. Don't ask. "There you are now," he coaxes his character. "[A]nd say what you're like, have a guess, what kind of man" (86). He pulls back, "too sudden, I gave myself a start," instantly projecting his palpitation, don't worry, "no one's going to love you and no one's going to kill you" (86). And then the dead flame ignites:

> I know how I'll do it, I'll be a man, there's nothing else for it, a kind of man, a kind of old tot, I'll have a nanny, I'll be her sweet pet . . . I'll be good, I'll sit quiet as a mouse in a corner and comb my beard. . . . She'll say to me, Come, doty, it's time for bye-bye. . . . her name will be Bibby, I'll call her Bibby. . . . Come, ducky, it's time for yum-yum. (86)

He drops it, wondering where such notions come from, the germs of fiction, and why the compulsion to project himself into characters. Then, "Quick quick before I weep" (87), and he is carried on inspiration:

> I'll have a crony, my own vintage, my own bog, a fellow warrior, we'll relive our campaigns and compare our scratches. Quick quick. . . . it's our positively last winter, halleluiah. . . . He's gone in the wind, I in the prostate. . . . I catheterize myself, unaided, with trembling hand, bent double in the public pisshouse. . . . We spend our life, it's ours, trying to bring together in the same instant a ray of sunshine and a free bench, in some oasis of public verdure. . . . No, alone, I'd be better off alone, it would be quicker. . . . he'd prevent discouragement from sapping my foundations. (87–88)

The spree ends with his swiping at it, as if clearing cobwebs from before his eyes, and with his blaming it on his condition of unbearable solitude. He speculates that his creative drive is a need to beget himself out of nothing—breath—words made flesh. "Departures, stories, they are not for tomorrow" (90). There are no tomorrows in his timeless space. "And the voices, wherever they come from, have no life in them" (90), not for him. He has taken a ride on his imagination and hopped off.

In *Text 4* he seeks the motive of his unstoppable urge to create. What drives the author to obsess on his characters? The narrator interrogates, speaking as the voice of a nascent character, "who says this, saying it's me?" (91). The narrator answers for him. "It's the same old stranger as ever, for whom alone accusative I exist" (91) as the object of the author's *let there be*, but no more in existence than the creative being of the author in its timeless solitude. "Forget me, know me not, yes, that would be the wisest, none better able than he" (91). You use me, you need me, ventriloquizes the narrator through his character, as if your death were due, and I'm there for your obscure longing. You, whose life is a continuous suicide, am I an atonement? "[M]ad, mad, he's mad. The truth is he's looking for me to kill me, to have me dead like him, dead like the living" (91).

This is shrewdly telling. There is no longer respite for the narrator in his unbearable nonexistence, making fictions. The ventriloquism continues. The voice asserts that it is not responsible for the narrator's enfeebled imagination, for the medley of hand-wringings that constitute his story, and it would seem his only story, which he repeats thirteen times for good measure, all the while insisting that it is not his story, there being nothing there where he is. "If at least he would dignify me with the third person, like his other figments, not he, he'll be satisfied with nothing less than me, for his me" (92).

The narrator's obsession with his characters has undergone a change. He wants release from the creative condition, the necessary condition for susceptibility to inspiration and to the making of stories. But that condition is his own nonexistence. Expending himself to create isn't worth it anymore. In truth he wants the godlike power to beget himself, to be the other, to exist as the other, which would be real respite. "[W]hat a thought," he ventriloquizes. "[T]reat him [the author] like that, like a vulgar Molloy, a common Malone, those mere mortals, happy mortals, have a heart, land him in that shit" (92).

The narrator discards his puppet. "What am I doing, talking, having my figments talk" (93). The simple answer is to render indelible the source of his malaise and exhaustion. He is sick to death of making stories. "What counts is to be in the world" (93). Lacking that longing, there can be no stories, and no place for him to go if he could go, and no one to be if he could be. He is exasperated by the persistence of his obsession with creativity.

The locus of *Text 5* is the narrator's effort to understand the origin of his guilt: "I'm the clerk, I'm the scribe, at the hearings of what cause I know not. Why want it to be mine, I don't want it. . . . To be judge and party, witness and advocate, and he, attentive, indifferent, who sits and notes" (95). The extended anal-

ogy to *The Trial* implies that the narrator feels like Joseph K.,
ambivalent, innocent and guilty, lawyer and executioner, "in the
silence of quite a different justice, in the toils of that obscure
assize where to be is to be guilty" (95), a part of him impatiently
drumming his fingers, quill in hand, taking it down.

"A cage went in search of a bird," says Kafka aphoristically,
perhaps about the futility of trying to get to the bottom of guilt.[8]
In *Text 5* the specimen feels increasingly enclosed "as it were
under glass" (97), and yet with no limit to his movements. "[L]et
him understand who can" (97). The allusion is to Dante in
Canto 9 of the *Inferno*, words obscurely underscoring a moral:
perhaps that the imagination in its compulsion to inquire par-
takes of sin in its quest for understanding. The tone of the narration hisses, not from sibilants, but perhaps from his feeling
cornered, persecuted. He considers that the trial is a divine summons to stand "before the justice of him who is all love, unforgiv-
ing and justly so, but subject to strange indulgences, the accused
will be my soul" (97). He mocks the notion, a thin sneer, unable
to make a joke of it: "It's tiring, very tiring, in the same breath to
win and lose, with concomitant emotions, one's heart is not of
stone, to record the doom, don the black cap and collapse in the
dock, very tiring, in the long run" (98).

The guilt and anxiety persist. He cannot account for them.
"It's a game, it's getting to be a game" (98). He imagines himself
walking away from his guilt, and that the image walking off is a
phantom, a file of phantoms accusing, deserting, haunting him.
He would attribute his guilt to a diseased imagination, that the
proceedings were all in his head. "That's where the court sits
this evening, in the depths of that vaulty night, that's where I'm
clerk and scribe, not understanding what I hear, not knowing
what I write" (98). Too late for prayers to be offered for his soul.
Better to have died unborn in the womb, when prayers have effi-
cacy. "[S]weet thing theology" (99). With morning, he wonders if
it must be the end of the session. Of his guilt, he has understood
no more than Joseph K.

In *Text 6* he tries to understand his prison and becomes increasingly bitter. "How are the intervals filled between these ap-
paritions? Do my keepers"—characters—"snatch a little rest
and sleep before setting about me afresh. . . . They like their

work, I feel it in my bones! No, I mean how filled for me, they don't come into this" (101). The only issue is I, how I survive the vacancy.

"Wretched acoustics this evening, the merest scraps, literally" (101). That is, nothing much happening, nothing with which to play. Yet he goes on to describe a searing memory, perhaps brought to mind by an associational link to scraps. "The news, do you remember the news, the latest news, in slow letters of light, above Piccadilly Circus, in the fog?" (101). Grief-stricken at the time and weary with crying, the narrator had forgotten where he was, though his eyes took in the moving column of news and the little tobacconist's shop. That kind of seeing without seeing is "far from common, on the whole" (101), he says, dropping the memory and returning to his investigations.

Why refer to his characters as "keepers" he asks. Because he is their prisoner, a prisoner of the compulsion to write. He remembers breaking down under the burden, the obsessional work and estrangement from life become horrifying, underworldly, undirected, ghoulish. The obsession with his keepers is like dwelling "elsewhere" in an "infinite here" (102), and he cannot get out. He cannot get out because he cannot stop engaging the creative impulse. If he could, "The air would be there again, the shadows of the sky drifting over the earth, and that ant, that ant" (102). There would not be phantoms, but something real. Instead, "look at me, a little dust in a little nook, stirred faintly this way and that by breath straying from the lost without" (102–103). But there's the rub, life among the living. Better his accursed life, "well pleased, that it's over and done with, the puffing and panting after me up and down their Tempe of tears" (103). A writer need only wipe it out, appeals to conscience and the rest.

"What can have become then of the tissues I was" (103), deliberately confusing his characters and persona in the real world. "Did I ever believe in them, did I ever believe I was there, somewhere in that ragbag" (103). What then of the memories, the boy of twelve looking at himself in the shaving glass, his father with him in the bathroom, and of the "view of the sea" (104) from the bathroom window, and of his mother who did her hair before the same mirror "with twitching hands" (104)?

"[W]hat a refreshing whiff of life on earth," he sneers dismissively (104).

Well, he had sacrificed all that, betrayed all that, and had paid for his calling, "Plunged in ice up to the nostrils, the eyelids caked with frozen tears" (104), had betrayed those ties and claims for "this thing, this farrago of silence and words, of silence that is not silence and barely murmured words. . . . this pell-mell babel of silence and words" (104). Toward what end? The simple answer, he says, is to tell a story, to get beyond himself—his sense of mockery and skepticism about the ability of language to affirm anything, of there being no quarry but only the hunt itself—and actually "tell a story, in the true sense of the words" (105). He has "high hopes," he says, "a little story, with living creatures coming and going on a habitable earth crammed with the dead" (105). The trailer is a snicker and another reversal.

In *Text 7* he accedes to despair. "Did I try everything, ferret in every hold, secretly, silently, patiently, listening? I'm in earnest, as so often, I'd like to be sure I left no stone unturned before reporting me missing and giving up" (107). Where is that deadbeat who is home and agent for the narrator in his creative trance, which is to say, where is the being that writes when not suspended between sleep and waking? Nowadays he is nonexistent when not writing, an absence passing like "an evening shadow" (107); nevertheless, agitated by memories, preyed upon, unspared, "come back it must with its riot of instants" (108), a hellish torture.

But, he protests, it is not to him the memories belong. They belong to "X," his pseudo-self,

> that paradigm of human kind, moving at will, complete with joys and sorrows, perhaps even a wife and brats, forbears most certainly, a carcass in God's image and a contemporary skull, but above all endowed with movement, that's what strikes you above all, with his likeness so easy to take and his so instructive soul . . . enough vile parrot I'll kill you. (108)

There follows a memorable image in double exposure representing the futility of a writerly ambition and the hellish despair of being one of the elect. He finds himself in the third-class waiting room of a train station, lost to the deafening echoes of departing trains, punishing memories revolving like the spokes of a turning wheel in his head. He is to be a writer, he can make no sense of anything unless he is writing, "so given am I to thinking with my breath" (109).

He imagines himself still sitting there, "hands on thighs, ticket between finger and thumb, in that great room dim with the platform gloom" (109), waiting in obedience to an inner compulsion "for a train that will never come, never go, natureward" (110). This is the ghostly counterpart of the double negative, that of his pensum, the station in ruins where he sits waiting, a shade among the dead, where day will never "break behind the locked door, through the glass black with the dust of ruin" (110). That is where the eye of his writing self is, where his soul waits when not hovering between dream and waking, until "night is at hand and the time come for me too to begin" (110).

In *Text 8* he laments not being able to stop his own voice, and so die. He seems cocooned in that "elsewhere," only sounds of the murmuring words in his head. He says he

> weep[s] too without interruption. It's an unbroken flow of words and tears. With no pause for reflection. . . . my words are my tears, my eyes my mouth. . . . it's for ever the same murmur, flowing unbroken, like a single endless word and therefore meaningless, for it's the end [the pauses and stops] gives the meaning to words. (111)

This is his "threne" (111), he says, he is buried alive, a hovering between life and death like some kind of hideous nightmare creature, droning to hear himself drone and straining to detect other voices. When did it happen to him, existing in a timeless space? Was it ever different? More than likely he had been expunged from life, or had "burrowed . . . out" or in, as it is, "till suddenly I was here" (112), and ever since, his pensum, to tell the story, a story of how he had gotten where he is and got out.

His hope is to be worn away, to wear out his head and his voice like a pebble ground to sand; or to "at least get out of here, at least that, no?" (112). He is not sure. He wants to live in time—he wants death—but is repelled by life's bewildered wretchedness. He wonders if he has been swallowed up by words and is in some ghastly prison. "If so let them open again and let me out, in the tumult of light that sealed my eyes, and of men, to try and be one again" (113). If his doom is a curse, he begs to "be forgiven and graciously authorized to expiate," above in the light, "every day a little purer, a little deader" (113). His doom seems inexplicable; he has offended no one. Yet he cannot be sure of anything that passes through his head; he may be "a mere ventriloquist's dummy" (113). Perhaps he is here because of "that other who is me," entombed "in this black silence, help-less to move or accept this voice as mine" (113), because of him whom he must impersonate until he dies. It is a ghastly alterna-tive, to be consciously dead in a fool's head or damned as he is. "[A]h if no were content to cut yes's throat and never cut its own" (113–14). In any case he has no say in the matter, or per-haps, like magic, the right aggregate of words will open his prison: "So as to be here no more at last, to have never been here, but all this time above, with a name like a dog . . . panting towards the grand apnoea" (114).

He imagines himself an old beggar with an ear trumpet hold-ing out a veined hand or hat at a terraced café, but drops the jeu d'esprit. "I would know it was not me, I would know I was here, begging in another dark, another silence, for another alm, that of being or of ceasing, better still, before having been" (115).

He evokes his desperate wish to be liberated through death in *Text 9.* "If I said, There's a way out there, there's a way out somewhere, the rest would come. What am I waiting for then, to say it? To believe it? And what does that mean, the rest?" (117). He despairs of ever getting out, of being other than a disembod-ied consciousness. It is the hell, perhaps, of the uninspired wait-ing for inspiration. The vacancy occupies him, the knowing of nothing for certain, the waiting, the panting sighs, the same re-curring thoughts, mechanical as the changing shapes of the moon. "[H]ow monotonous. What agitation and at the same time what calm, what vicissitudes within what changelessness," man-aging by means of "the old crux," word play (118). "That's right, wordshit, bury me, avalanche, and let there be no more talk of any creature, nor of a world to leave, nor of a world to reach, in order to have done, with worlds, with creatures, with words, with misery, misery" (118). Words are tears, words extruded under torture; his mouth is his eyes. Yet he has nothing else but words to keep him going, allowing him to hope to die, liberated. "I'd have a mother, I'd have had a mother. . . . here are my tomb and mother, it's all here this evening, I'm dead and getting born, without having ended, helpless to begin, that's my life" (118–19).

Words, tears, musings, shit, whether risen or rotten, changes nothing for him. Fame is shit to him who lives buried alive, knowing nothing for certain, mouthing like a cretin.

From his limbo of tormented, impatient consciousness he projects himself into a Molloy-like bum, solely for the savor of mortality, the proximity of oblivion. No possession occurs. The projection is little more than a flight. The losing of self into the bum's fearful suspicion that he is being watched by unfriendly eyes will not do or is beyond him. Oblivion absorbs him, the image of himself "slinking to and fro before the graveyard" (119). Is he, can he, was he, will he be, is that he, a mortal? How is he to believe it? No "shudders and wry faces" (119) betray his presence.

He occupies himself imagining "proof positive" (119) for the existence of the bum, occupying himself with that as if it were a plan of escape, as if, by the spell of these proof positives, he might eject himself into the other being and be on the road of ceasing to be.

This is desperation. Other things at other times occupy his musings. "The way out, this evening it's the turn of the way out" (117).

> [I]f I could get out of here . . . there's a way out somewhere, to know exactly where would be a mere matter of time, and patience, and sequency of thought, and felicity of expression. . . . if I could say, There's a way out there, there's a way out somewhere, the rest would come, the other words, sooner or later, and the power to get there, and the way to get there, and pass out, and see the beauties of the skies, and see the stars again. (121)

So rises a silent prayer for mercy.

In *Text 10*, he thinks almost playfully of his undying yes to the creative drive. "Give up, but it's all given up, it's nothing new. . . . never anything, but giving up. But let us suppose" (123). Mocking himself, his head again "slobbering its shit" (123), he cozies up to the notion "that one day I shall know again that I once was, and roughly who, and how to go on, and speak unaided, nicely, about number one and his pale imitations" (124). He takes the hook greedily for want of distraction. Maybe he is "being licked into shape" along with "other souls," barely usable, for reassignment "to flesh, as the dead are committed to the ground" (124). He dilates on the wreckage he'd be cast among, and peters out. His heart isn't in it. "No, no souls, or bodies, or birth, or life, or death, you've got to go on without any of that junk" (125).

Until "another guzzle of lies but piping hot" (125). That's survival, "giving up, that's it, I'll have gone on giving up, having had nothing, not being there" (125). This is a lighter take on his ambivalence, even wry.

Against a plangent note of sadness, *Text 11* wittily evokes the irrepressible yes to his creative drive, still occasionally sparking. No, he says to yes, pretending to be the Molloylike bum, "no, that won't work" (127), but he pretends it anyway. But his words are not his; he is merely their dummy. Proofs that he exists in the mortal world are theirs; their words are "premature" (128). "But peekaboo here I come again, just when most needed . . . the livid face stained with ink and jam, caput mortuum of a studious youth . . . foaming at the mouth, and chewing" (128).

The boy in the course of the description of the gob in his mouth turns into "a snotty old nipper, having terminated his humanities" (129) in a public bathroom. It is definitely he at the urinal, his mortal self, drunk and straining against an enlarged prostate, definitely. The gurgling of the urinal reminds him of his mother encouraging him to pee when he was a baby on the pot. "I invent nothing," he says (129). He's priming himself for the exfoliation: "erect on my trusty stumps, bursting with old piss, old prayers, old lessons, soul, mind and carcass finishing neck and neck," hawking up his heart in a convulsive sob, dying, dying, "Jesus, Jesus" (129).

Such self-dramatization is beyond him now; he can't pull that off anymore, "when I used to say, from within, or from without, from the coming night or from under the ground, Where am I" (129). Gone from himself into other beings, stories. Now, prattle, prattling on, questions that lead nowhere, heartless surmises, compared to which, "those were the days, I didn't know where I was, nor in what semblance, nor since when, nor till when, whereas now, there's the difference" (130). He can only muster a kind of stitching and unstitching, yesing his nos, petering on. "[Y]es, a new no, that none says twice, whose drop will fall and let me down, shadow and babble, to an absence less vain than inexistence" (131).

But he can't relinquish himself to a naked no. "[S]omewhere above in their gonorrhoeal light" (131), he doesn't believe it, he spots himself among others who know him, and splits himself in two, a "no" persona receding into solitude and a "yes" persona moving on in the company of the others. "[T]hat is all I can have had to say, this evening" (131).

Text 12 is an aborted prayer for something finer, better than existence, which he cannot bear.

> It's a winter night, where I was, where I'm going, remembered, imagined, no matter, believing in me, believing it's me . . . but on earth, beyond all doubt on earth, for as long as it takes to die again, wake again, long enough for things to change here, for something to change, to make possible a deeper birth, a deeper death, or resurrection in and out of this murmur of memory and dream. (133)

He spots himself, momentarily projects himself into the mind of a character he constructs, then backs off and regards the old veteran "muttering, the old inanities" (134), he (the bum) a wreck, and he (the author) the usurper. He backs off, repelled by "the shame of my living that kept me from living" (134). The effort to inhabit a mortal and move toward death is undercut by the abhorrence of being mortal.

Interrogatives continue. Who's raving, whose voices, who's listening, a kind of word-slinging hypnosis for the ejection into the other and simultaneous holding back, hesitation before birth, a rallying now, "none ever waited to die for me to live in him, so as to die with him . . . quick quick" (134). Yet no quickening possession of the other, no slipping in of memories and dreams, no stories from him.

So, I'm supposed to say now, it's the moment, so that's the earth, these expiring vitals set aside for me . . . many thanks. . . . what a blessing it's all down the drain, nothing ever as much as begun, nothing ever but nothing and never, nothing ever but lifeless words. (134–35)

In *Text 13*, the turmoil goes on, hatred of life sapping his imaginative drive, torment in isolation waking his creativity. If there is no inspiration to create characters and their stories, there is nothing. Such is the import of "the weak old voice that tried in vain to make me, dying away as much as to say it's going from here to try elsewhere . . . it's going to cease, give up trying. . . . if not of life, there it dies" (137).

A primary motive of the creative drive is to leave a trace. "A trace, it wants to leave a trace" (137). It is out of the feeling for life that it would make a life. But he's devoid of the feeling. He cannot bear the endeavor, propitiating for inspiration that is merely respite before the falling back into himself. He cannot get it on because he cannot get out of where he is. "[H]ow when here is empty" (138).

Why does it linger on, the faint will to create? "But what more is it waiting for now, when there's no doubt left, no choice left, to stick a sock in its death-rattle, yet another locution. To have rounded off its cock-and-bullshit in a coda worthy of the rest?" (139).

He goes on abusing his writerly imagination and the motive of his being, striking blows for "the extinction of this black nothing and its impossible shades, the end of the farce of making and the silencing of silence" (139). No more teasing, he pronounces, "ended, we're ended who never were, soon there will be nothing where there was never anything" (139).

He cannot stop. Enraged bitterness at the deception, the swallowing of lies—that from shit and darkness the soul slowly wakes, flashing forth like a point of light, and in the virgin womb of the imagination the word is made flesh—uplifts him in a frenzy. And still "the screaming silence of no's knife in yes's wound" (139), unkillable yes, irrepressible yes to the windless hour of dawn when madness wakes and the seraph comes to the virgin chamber. "And were there one day to be here, where there are no days, which is no place, born of the impossible voice the unmakable being, and a gleam of light" (140). Caught up in the mystery of "In the beginning was the Word," it is impossible fully to imagine nonbeing.

Each text is a different gambit in a sequence generated out of a nexus of unbearable, contradictory desires—to live in the world, to live in the imagination—which is the plight of the writer and the source of his creativity. Each text has its own emotional curve, its shape of feelings, and the sequence itself is carried by the momentum of its always changing register. *Texts 1* and *2* contradict each other; he takes refuge in his imagination, he cannot make the effort to live through his imagination. Yet the drive persists, which he mocks in *Text 3*. In *4* he seeks the motive of the unstoppable urge, and in *5* evokes the guilt and anxiety connected with that motive. In *6* he oscillates between the two unbearable poles, life and imaginative life. He evokes his despair as a writer in *7*, and the torture of an unceasing consciousness in *8*. *Text 9* evokes his desperation, in an allusion to Dante emerging from hell, his plea for mercy. In *10* he tries to make light of the unstoppable folly of yesing the no to his going on. *Text 11* is a jaunty evocation of the irrepressible yes, still sparking. *Text 12* is an abortive prayer for something better than life, and in *13* the tumult goes on as ever: hatred of life sapping his imaginative drive, torment and isolation waking his creativity.

The shape is the voice in its different moods describing and lamenting its predicament. The arc traveled through the sequence is not to an achieved change at the end because no change is conceivable. The aim of *Texts* is futile, which is to say, there can be no transformative aim because of the nature of the artist. His inspiration depends on the separation from life and the contradictory longing to be in the world he despises. If he joined the world he would cease to exist as a writer. In despising the world, he ceases to exist as a writer. He is condemned to observe and to oscillate, desiring the unbearable in an inferno of shifting moods that is his imaginative life. In the end, the only way to escape is not to have been. But he cannot die because he goes on living in the texts he creates, which is the reason he creates them. He continues to exist posthumously but laments this existence.

There is a baffling sense of discomfort that does not let up. This is not ennui but terrible engagement. Life has become "Prometheus Bound" without the transformative vision, just as in Kafka we live in a Pauline universe without a God.

Here, being an artist is not transformative. The artist has no sense of superiority and no claims are made for art. The *Texts* are an assault on the life waste that goes into writing. They demolish the artistic pose while attesting to an unstoppable urge.

6
Playing Past the Endgame

After the impasse depicted in *Texts for Nothing*, Beckett's art illuminates a revivifying discovery: the self wishes to be engaged with another self in the interest of pain. The tortuous deadlock evoked in *Texts for Nothing* may have fed into this discovery. Doomed in that station at a crossroads where the choices are deadening, the creative imagination dims as if dying out. Yet it is impossible to imagine it dead; it continuously recrudesces: the self-torturing impasse that brought Kafka to the edge of madness in 1922—sick, despairing, exhausted—nevertheless and miraculously roused his imagination into bringing forth *The Castle*.

When Beckett wrote *Texts*, he was searching for a way to advance his art in new directions by looking back to his struggle with spiritual deadlock in 1946, when with Kafka's help he made the transition from the *Nouvelles* to the trilogy. That new direction is the discovery of the importance of torture to the imagination. In *Texts*, the writer's imagination continuously reanimates itself under the stimulation of self-torture. As perceived in *Endgame* and in *How It Is*, the spur to creativity expands to include the torture of others—*a* to *b*, *b* to *c*, *c* to *d*, in an infinitely expandable line of torturers and victims. In the transformative vision of *How It Is*, the quickening of life itself is all a matter of stinging and being stung—human existence likened to an endless track of beetles, each biting the one ahead and being bitten from behind. Obliging the human species to show its beetle face revivifies Beckett. We live in a world of matter and pain; it is all *Inferno*, or, rather, more specific to

Beckett, the world of the concentration camp. *Endgame*'s "hooks" get below the bearable surface, with its irreproachable ethic, ordered lifestyle, and exemplary behavior, to where satisfaction lies in possessing the soul of another, and control—sadistic violation—is a primal law of creation.

On a more immediate level, *Endgame* creates the spectacle of what it takes to face one's dying undiminished. There can be no mercy; going "gently" is being alive in a postmortem drool of nostalgia and pain. In *Malone Dies*, Malone writes because there is the illusion in writing that nothing can happen unless I say so. In *Endgame* Hamm goes one better. He negates time itself. He exists in the moment and invents himself anew in each successive moment. So long as he performs, nothing terrible can become real. One supposes that even Death is dazzled by the play of the blind paralytic propped up in his wheelchair, forestalling despair with his countermoves, while we, the audience, look on in awe at his outrageousness. So this is what it would take to say, fuck all and make the most of what is left. His parents in ashcans spotlight his freedom from compunction. There are no anchors, only the absolutely indispensable dragline to Clov, his rebellious servant-son, who opens the curtain, soliloquizing.

"[I]t must be nearly finished,"[9] for "[g]rain upon grain, one by one" Clov has also grown into an invalid, lame and stooped. "[S]uddenly, there's a heap, a little heap, the impossible heap." What worse can life do to him? "I can't be punished any more" (1). It is too late to change, and how his hair is growing thin! "I'll go now to my kitchen, ten feet by ten feet by ten feet, and wait for him to whistle me" (2). Because Clov takes shelter in the mental space created by the dying Hamm, his world is postapocalyptic.

Hamm wakes immediately conscious of the necessity of a countermove to stay the hemorrhaging towards despair. Why go on? He is "[o]ld stancher" (2)! He yawns at the consciousness of his misery, and further removes himself from it by finding comparison with other renowned sufferers, cues for performance. He whistles for Clov, scorning his servant's mewling efforts to leave him, and says in greeting, "You pollute the air!" (3) meaning, how much of this can you take; meaning, dog, be a man and finish me off. Hamm is not bluster; he is pure occasion. He seizes on what is given him for invention, play. Clov's threat of abandoning him is a stimulus to needle and knead the dull dough of his servant. "I've made you suffer too much. (*Pause.*) Haven't I? . . . I haven't made you suffer too much? . . . Ah you gave me a fright! . . . Why don't you kill me?" (6–8).

Clov falls into step, the servant and straight man. "I'll leave you" (9), he says, a weak threat because immediately clarified— I'll withdraw to the kitchen to wait for your whistle. Sounds from the parents elicit from Clov a reflection: "No one that ever lived ever thought so crooked as we." Hamm: "We do what we can." Clov: "We shouldn't"—a joke. Hamm: "You're a bit of all right, aren't you?" Clov: "A smithereen" (11–12). They guffaw together at the absurdity of moral restraints.

Nagg knocks for Nell. "What is it, my pet? (*Pause.*) Time for love?" (14). The pathos of infantile dependence, peeing and defecating in bed, cribbed. Dribblers, spooning pap and dreaming of bonbons. Never that for Hamm, no mercy on himself. Hamm's heart is bleeding in his head in order not to be like that. "There's something dripping in my head. (*Pause.*) A heart" (18). That's what it takes to ride the anxiety of dying. "My kingdom for a nightman!" (23). Perhaps an allusion to Richard III, who gorged on his own heart. This is what it takes to be a king in the staged space of one's dying. "Take me for a little turn" (25), he commands. His ferocious egotism fascinates the audience.

Clov: "If I could kill him I'd die happy" (27). He means, if he could break his dependency and his fear of the outside, he would abandon Hamm.

Hamm provokes a test of strength. "What's the weather like?" "As usual." "Look at the earth." "I've looked." "With the glass?" "No need of the glass." "Look at it with the glass" (27–28). Clov does his bidding, going through the motions as if mentally retarded, mocking himself and exasperating Hamm. Hamm orders him to scan the view from the oceanside. Zero, gray, thrice gray: earth dead, ocean dead, sun dead. There is nowhere for Clov to escape. He screams the word "[g]ray" (31) in the violence of his deflation.

Hamm makes a joke. "We're not beginning to . . . to . . . mean something?" (32)—aiming for a mutual guffaw, a strategic move to give leverage back to Clov in order to keep the dance going. Clov laughs bitterly. "Mean something!" (33)—grain upon grain until a heap, then ransacked, ravaged, then nothing.

To escape time, Hamm forbids contexts. He wills himself to have no memory. Memories, regrets, mean living half-submerged. Hamm shifts the balance of power in order to give the flow of energy to Clov, who kills a flea with zest. Clov: "What about that pee?"—meaning, shall I get the catheter? Hamm: "I'm having it." Clov: "Ah that's the spirit" (34), as if ready for anything.

Hamm fantasizes that they go off together on a raft "far away, to other . . . mammals!" Clov: "God forbid!" Hamm, instantaneous: "Alone, I'll embark alone! Get working on that raft immediately." Not a trace of recoil from that rebuff. "Tomorrow I'll be gone for ever." Clov: "I'll start straight away" (34–35). Hamm reels him in: "You can't leave us. . . . Why don't you finish us? . . . Do you remember when you came here? . . . It was I was a father to you. . . . My house a home for you. . . . But for me, (*gesture towards himself*) no father. But for Hamm, (*gesture towards surroundings*) no home" (37–38). Then he baits him. After working on his fear that out there is death, that out there he would be like a grit of dirt in the middle of a steppe, Hamm says, "Did you ever think of one thing? . . . That here we're down in a hole. (*Pause.*) But beyond the hills? Eh? Perhaps it's still green. . . . Perhaps you won't need to go very far" (39). And then he mocks Clov, reducing him to a dog gazing up at him in supplication, utterly defeated for the moment in a struggle that for Hamm must not end.

Dangerously, daringly, Hamm tells a story, a parable, in which a man (Clov) is trapped in a state of mind, a mental aberration. A friend (Hamm) would visit him at the asylum and point out from the window the loveliness of the world. But the lunatic would snatch his hand away and go back into his corner, "Appalled. All he had seen was ashes. (*Pause.*) He alone had been spared. (*Pause.*) Forgotten (44)." Just the opposite has been Hamm's treatment of Clov. Hamm has turned him into something analogous to the lunatic: fearful of life. Implicitly the parable remarks on the fate of a man enchanted within a world that is the mind-set of a dying man. Implicitly, Hamm's parable translates into, *I have imprisoned you, Clov*. Then he continues to taunt Clov, who has turned to leave, perhaps this time for good. "Do you not think this has gone on long enough? . . . This . . . this . . . thing" (45)—that is, this dance of theirs that keeps Hamm going and Clov from going. He dares Clov to abandon him every time Clov starts to leave; every trip to the kitchen is occasion for Hamm to defy his own fear of abandonment. Then, gravely, as if his life depends on the answer, he asks how he is to know whether Clov left or just dropped dead in the kitchen from the fear of leaving.

Clov considers the matter with equal gravity. He will set the alarm to the clock before leaving. If Hamm hears the alarm, he will know that Clov is either gone or dead. Clov tests the alarm. The power flows to him, a note of jubilation, gaiety, and hard ferocity enters his rebuffs.

Hamm's countermove is to introduce his "chronicle," the verses pertaining to the genesis of Clov: earth cursed, its populations dead or dying, a suppliant prostrate in the dust before him. The man begs for food for his dying child. Hamm offers the man refuge. The man pleads for him to take the child. Hamm intends a rebuff. "It was the moment I was waiting for" (53). Self-dramatization, Hamm posing as the monster bastard for the freedom it confers, and to stick it to Clov. See me, that's me. So hate me, and up yours, keeping a step ahead of his fear of abandonment and death. Clov becomes the enraged bull gracefully maneuvered.

Clov stomps about the stage putting things in order with a vengeance, acting out a prelude to departure. Hamm: "What's wrong with your feet? . . . Tramp! Tramp!" Clov: "I must have put on my boots" (57–58). To keep Clov from leaving, Hamm resumes his chronicle of how God saved Clov from among innumerable suppliants for mercy. Cancel. The real story is how God in his greater wisdom denied mercy, mercy to all in the blight that is life, but chose the father and the brat to survive a little longer, to be gardeners (Clov howls with laughter) on a planet of ashes. I took you in, Clov, goes the story, against reason and compassion, as my son.

Suddenly he snaps, "Go and see is she dead" (62). Nell is dead in her garbage can. Nagg is crying, reports Clov. Hamm takes the cue: "Then he's living" (62). And then somehow the space seems to open out, the board is cleared. Hamm, more desperately alone, delivers a funeral oration on the text of heartless bastards:

> All those I might have helped. (*Pause.*) Helped! (*Pause.*) Saved. (*Pause.*) Saved! (*Pause.*) The place was crawling with them! (*Pause. Violently.*) Use your head, can't you, use your head, you're on earth, there's no cure for that! (*Pause.*) Get out of here and love one another! Lick your neighbor as yourself! (*Pause. Calmer.*) When it wasn't bread they wanted it was crumpets. (*Pause. Violently.*) Out of my sight and back to your petting parties! (68–69)

Weakening, is he? Tears for his mother drawn forth by guilt at his treatment of her? How live within the slaughterhouse of life? Run a soup kitchen where there are a hundred thousand starving and soup for a hundred? A Bible school, a crocheting party for mothers? It is not worth the trouble, Heartless Bastard God, to be born.

He whistles for Clov. Clov is in psychic uproar, acting out a determination and gaiety he does not feel in his guts. He is not in the clear. No more pain pills, he gleefully tells Hamm. Hamm screams (one recalls Kafka's words when begging Klopstock for morphine and thinking he's holding back: "Kill me, or you're a murderer."[10]). Clov sings triumphantly. Hamm orders him again to scan the world with the glass. He pleads, "What has happened?" (75)—meaning, am I really out of moves? Clov shouts at him for telling Mother Pegg to go to hell when she came begging. Clov literally pants from the effort to break loose.

Hamm: "Oh you won't find it easy" (76). Clov, pleading: "Let's stop playing!" (77)—meaning, let me go, help me to go. Hamm: "Never!" (77). I will not resign myself to death.

What is one to make of the boy Clov spies from the window, shouting the discovery? Is he an imagined replacement for Clov? But instead of rallying at the evidence that life can exist outside the shelter, his instantaneous reaction is to grab the gaff. The boy must be killed: a potential procreator. Clov has gone completely over to Hamm's point of view.

Hamm pounces on this evidence of weakness. "It's the end, Clov, we've come to the end. I don't need you any more" (79). This is a complex move. He orders Clov to give him the gaff. Do not harm the boy, the way is clear for you. I don't put it past you to leave me and prevent my survival by killing the boy. Go in peace. Only, tell me what you feel before you go. "A few words . . . to ponder . . . in my heart" (79). Hamm gives Clov the push he has begged for, but it's only to make Clov face his own cowardice.

But Clov is not buying. Something has run its course. I finally can leave you. "How easy it is," he says (80). I had thought this was life, I was safe. "Here's the place" (80). It was not so bad for all those dying outside, I thought. And then I thought the matter for me was to get used to suffering, that this existence here was a trial, and that if I were better at it one day I would be let go. Then one day I realized I had become too old to change and that I would never go. "Then one day, suddenly, it ends. . . . I open the door of the cell and go" (81). But does he really go? Or does he continue to wait by the unlocked door, like the man from the country in Kafka's parable, "The Man Before the Law," found in *The Trial*?

Hamm pretends to acquiesce. "I'm obliged to you, Clov. For your services" (81). Clov returns the courtesy and withdraws. Hamm shifts among selves, fragmented, raises hat, tries his hand at writing a line of poetry, entertains a philosophical paradox. These are all the poses of a desperate man. He resumes his chronicle: "You want [your brat] to bloom while you are withering? . . . He doesn't realize, all he knows is hunger, and cold, and death to crown it all. But you! You ought to know what the earth is like, nowadays. Oh I put him before his responsibilities!" (83). The merciful thing to do, given the state of the world, would have been to let the boy die. But Hamm took him in. Hamm became a father to Clov!

Hamm whistles long and loud for Clov. He screams for his father. He whimpers for Clov, who stands watching him, attired for departure, motionless. Hamm discards gaff and whistle, and covers his face with his blood-stained handkerchief. "Old stancher! (*Pause.*) You . . . remain" (84).

The play self-consciously calls attention to performance. Hamm's self-parody is another way of keeping the despair about dying at a distance. Hamm's stage persona keeps him from getting maudlin or hysterical. The only object is to get it up, the will to play, to go on and keep it going. To be vigilant like Malone and never to let one's guard down: "I feel the old dark gathering, the solitude preparing, by which I know myself, and the call of that ignorance which might be noble and is mere poltroonery" (*Malone Dies*).[11]

Poltroonery: a synonym for conscience as commonly understood. Hamm's way has been to effect a split between the rational, analytical cast of his mind and his emotions, as if cutting a central nerve and so dissociating his consciousness from the emotional base of his conscience. Survival depends on his not knowing himself and his emotions. He still has emotions—in fact at a threshold of sensations that is extreme—but the source of the stimulus has become impossible to locate. His performances—his survival—depend on his maintaining the split; at the same time, his performances tend to locate the stimulus and regenerate the severed nerve—a renewed connection that will destroy him. So in acting out his freedom—in fighting to survive—he is in danger of rediscovering his humanity and condemning himself. This is the theme of Pat Barker's World War I trilogy, *Regeneration*, *The Eye in the Door*, and *The Ghost Road*.

"Very pretty": the desire for validation and justice is suicidal in a world in which shell shock is a survival tactic and its cure is to go back to the trenches. The play within the play is the catastrophe life, endlessly repeated until rigor mortis sets in.

The curtain lifts on the hell that is the posthumous life of a survivor, one like that of the ape in Kafka's "A Report to an Academy," determined to survive death in captivity: "[O]ne learns when one needs a way out; one learns at all costs. One stands over oneself with a whip; one flays oneself at the slightest opposition."[12]

The Kafka story can be read as the story of Hamm's transformation. Survival means shedding his innate nature. It means watching himself with a whip in his hand. It is living as if on stage. Death waits in the wings playing Bach, amused by the Jew ape, the clown capo and his brood who are half insane with terror. It is their smell that repels Hamm, the bewildered, half-broken animal smell of his parents, a human odor still faintly traceable on himself.

Endgame lifts the curtain on the kind of hell found in a concentration camp: all existence leveled to a life that is itself death, dazed mass conformity. The choice is between the mussulman and the survivor, between being comatose or living with death; living with death means choosing violence and even murder, daring to murder to rid oneself of cowardice, daring to live engaged in segments of time present, each segment of time lived as one final battle, every social restraint removed, pulsing energy found in the psychopathy of an egoism tigerish in its abandonment. Hamm too is one of death's minions, crippled, blind clown. He can't go on, the game is over, the king and queen already taken; moves are pointless, there can't be a countermove. And still he goes on, playing to rid himself of his humanity with its air of ersatz happiness and smell of corpses.

7
Torturer and Servant,
or *How It Is*

H*ow It Is* (*Comment c'est*) is a difficult and puzzling text which has elicited numerous approaches from critics. A number of them view the novel through the lens of philosophy, focusing, for example, on Beckett's relationship to Sartre, or Camus; the Beckett/Geulincx connection; or on the influence of Democritus of Abdera.[13] Others concentrate on Beckett's use of the *Inferno*,[14] or read the novel as an illustration of Beckettian aesthetics by drawing on his critical statements in "Three Dialogues" and in his essays on painters. These aestheticians underscore the vain compulsion to impose unity and meaning on human experience through art[15] or see *How It Is* as a representation of the artist's struggle against, and submission to, suicide.[16] The novel is also seen as the creation through torture of a social being.[17]

Nearer to my own reading, Frederik N. Smith (1983) describes Beckett's attempts to catch the flux of the writing process as it happens. The contest is between imagination (spontaneous creation) and revision. However, Smith does not go beyond his argument that the novel represents the genesis of literary production.[18] There is no showing the story behind the story, or the story itself, which is my interest here.

Kafka's remark about the books we need points out the hole in commentaries on *How It Is*, which certainly has the requisite "bite and sting" of immediacy Kafka desires:

> If a book we're reading doesn't wake us up with a punch on the
> head, what are we reading it for? . . . We need the books which

116

affect us like a disaster, which pain us deeply, like the death of someone dearer to us than ourselves, like being lost in the woods, far from everyone, like a suicide, a book must be the axe for the frozen sea in us.[19]

The commentaries on *How It Is* seem unrevealing—object-less—because they provide no center of coherence; after reading the critics, one still has no sense of the novel, which Beckett thought of as "little book all my own the heart's outpourings."[20]

For me, Beckett's novel-length monologue resembles a medieval wall painting of the Last Judgment, but one that bears witness to the absence of redemption. As creator, the male speaker lives in a primordial world of mud and darkness, outside life, listening to the voice of his thoughts and beseeching that voice, as if external to his consciousness, to allow him to participate in the creative process. The novel represents this process symbolically as a four-stage cycle. In part 3, where the novel begins, he is in that no-man's-land of mud and darkness between the discarded finished work and the hoped-for, newly conceived one. Inspiration depends on his being able to draw on the power of a nexus of memories; his life has contracted into one implicit story—that of his wife's suicide and of his subsequent dereliction. The cycle of his creative process symbolically reenacts his guilt and punishment.

In part 1 he recounts the innocent first stage of the foreordained cycle, or journey to the main event: the discovery of his calling. The memories in this stage are disconnected because they precede his wife's suicide, the wellspring of his inspiration. With Pim (in part 2) he reenacts the torment he inflicted on his wife because he wants to reconnect with the persona that drove her to suicide. With Bom (in part 4) he relives the degradation he pursued, both as a retribution and as a means to cross the threshold of a new creation.

He creates art out of necessity because he exists only in his creations. *How It Is* is the story behind the story, the symbolic representation of the process by which he not only produces his fiction, but continues to exist. He finds no consolation in what he writes; he seeks none. All he wants is the impetus to sustain a new fiction, a fiction that inadvertently possesses, on occasion, redeeming value. It is leavened in this hell with the shit and vomit of the artist himself and of those he martyrs in his service to art.

Beyond this story of the writer's relationship to the fiction he produces, there is another, much more broad in scope. This is an apocalyptic vision of life as an impulsion to torture in order to be quickened, to be wakened, to be. The artist as witness and bearer of the tale discovers the human pageant in himself while begging the muse for reentrance into the process of torture by which he produces his art and sustains his existence.

Beckett wrote *How It Is* in French during a period of eighteen months throughout 1959 and into the summer of 1960. His biographer James Knowlson emphasizes Beckett's dedicated struggle with the text, which would come to fill five notebooks: a dozen lines or so a day, at most three hours of concentrated work—an absorption undistracted by any other writing. The book was published in 1961, the English translation by the author in 1964.

In a letter to Donald McWhinnie in April 1960, Beckett sketched the idea of the novel as follows:

> A "man" is lying panting in the mud and dark murmuring his "life" as he hears it obscurely uttered by a voice inside him. This utterance is described throughout the work as the fragmentary recollection of an extraneous voice once heard "quaqua on all sides." In the last pages he is obliged to take the onus of it on himself and of the lamentable tale of things it tells. The noise of his panting fills his ears and it is only when this abates that he can catch and murmur forth a fragment of what is being stated within. The work is in three parts, the first a solitary journey in the dark and mud terminating with discovery of a similar creature known as Pim, the second life with Pim both motionless in the dark and mud terminating with departure of Pim, the third solitude motionless in the dark and mud. It is in the third part that occur[s] the so-called voice "quaqua," its interiorisation and murmuring forth when the panting stops. That is to say the "I" is from the outset in the third part and the first and second, though stated as heard in the present, already over. (quoted in Knowlson 413)

Although the narrator of *How It Is* is unnamed, we may safely call him M. Most of Beckett's major characters have names beginning with M; *M* is to Beckett as *K* is to Kafka. M is a solitary consciousness uncertain of the source of his own thoughts. Terror inspires his belief in the externality of a voice that he can imperfectly hear as if inside his head. From nothing, or, rather, from the panicky fear of his being nothing more than a consciousness without creative power, he invents a voice and imagines a former time when there were others in the mud with him, attentive to the same voice, murmuring its words; for he could hear their collective murmur or "quaqua" (*How It Is*, 7) all about him. From this starting point of an external voice, the narrator creates and peoples a fictional world—an apocalyptic world like that of soldiers dying in the mud of no-man's-land between the trenches, murmuring their prayers. This hell is also retributive, the enactment of a symbolic judgment. Guilt is tacitly acknowledged in the nature of the punishment. M continuously relives and retells a fictionalized version of his crimes and punishments as he is recycled through the four stages of his torment. His art rises out of mud and darkness only when he is able to reenter the cycle of torment.

The novel, seen from outside, is the fable of the artist's creative process. It is invented out of nothing, mud and darkness—which is to say, the cycle of M's torment is no less his fiction than the fiction he creates by its process; he must create the method as well as its product. Murmuring to the mud, the point of nothingness from which invention proceeds, becomes a stage (part 3) in the cycle, a period of cognizance when he is given to understand by the voice the special features of his life in the mud. It is as a *conoscente*, one endowed with understanding, that he tells this story, and the fiction is upheld by the teller's total engagement. He effects this feeling of passionate engagement by narrating the past in the present tense, layering on the journeyer's sensuous awakening and innocent transit (part one) his own bitterness of thought and feeling, so overriding the narrative with his charged commentary that it is necessary to help readers situate themselves with other devices. He does this most notably by means of formulaic phrases. "[T]his sack this slime the mild air the black dark the coloured images the power to crawl" (22) and "the cord sawing my neck the sack jolting at my side" (16). These are leitmotifs for the journey, musically recurring in variations. Similar motifs identify each of the other stages in the cycle. The frequent repetition and variety of these formulaic phrases also indicate an element of pride in the artistry of the design.

M must uphold imagination against the fact of maddening solitude. At a point of emptiness in the symbolic representation of the process by which fiction is produced, M prays to the muse for a trickle more of the necessary plasma of guilt and disgust. He needs to milk his life for the memories that are always at the heart of the matter of whatever he produces. As journeyer, "bits and scraps" (7) of his former "life in the light" (9) gleam and fade out. They come and go, become motifs, are announced by a single phrase, a word. They return in part 2 through Pim's voice, and are available to the *conoscente* who remembers what he saw.

His wife's fall or jump from a window and his going to pieces are the central events of his life. The floodgates open to these memories through Pim, whom he bloodies and plays like his instrument in order to force him to tell of his, M's, life. In the retelling Pim takes the place of M's wife, so that M can experience himself again driving another to suicide. As artist he can only tap into the power of those events by reenacting them. Hardly a detail from that core of memory engages M's commentary on the journey—a glimpse of his wasted life "at the small hour of the garbage-man" (37), and one persistent, recurring memory that easily knits in to the implicit story. He sees a woman who is sewing or embroidering watching him sitting at a table, perhaps writing. His head rests motionless on the table, his hand trembles. She grows frightened. She knows he is not sleeping; she does not call; he does not move. She suddenly runs from the house. The memory returns with haunting persistence: the dead head, the living hand, the woman fleeing. As a prelude to the main event, the memory has an odious suggestiveness. Possibly there is no aspect of their relationship that is not torture.

There are other memories, but only those pertaining to his wife's suicide and his flight from himself sustain his fiction. We might isolate one alchemical moment in the artistry by which guilty memory is transformed into punishing judgment, or, his former life into life in the mud. "[W]hat have I done where been

that kind mute screams abandon hope gleam of hope frantic departure the cord round my neck the sack in my mouth a dog"
(46). This appears to be a close transcription of his wife's suicide
and its sequel. His "mute screams" and "abandon[ed] hope" on
hearing of her death, his "gleam of hope" in her lingering on at
the hospital, his "frantic departure" indicating flight from himself. The "sack" and "cord" are his only possessions in drunken
vagrancy. "Dog" has all kinds of evocations: panting like a dog;
from behind like a dog. He is to Pim as Bom is to him, enacting a
self-punishing retribution in sodomy. In the sequel to his wife's
suicide, M becomes Bom's Bom. "[I]t will be my first Bom he can
call me Bom/ . . . you can shit on a Bom sir you can't humiliate
him" (60). He permits himself to be used by anybody.

It is not accountability for his life, moral understanding, the
conoscente wants. Each time, recycled through the agonizing
process, he has to rebuild the edifice of his hell and mine his
memories for the new fiction. Concentration and faith in his
imagination are wanted in the face of nonexistence. Speculating
on his torment, whether it is everlasting or whether there is
hope for change, makes for "good moments" (23). Massaging the
conception is reassuring; the body of faith is there. Was there a
time when the sack contained refreshing necessities, when he
had other needs, "the wish for a little beauty" (12)? He imagines
himself as journeyer combing his hair, blowing it dry, and fluff-
ing it up. He recalls his "golden age" days (47). Peace for him is
being in the flux of the writing process at the moment it happens. Blaspheming the wickedness of his hellish conception also
affords him a measure of peace.

There is one sweet memory among the five or six that constitute M's former life. A child kneels in prayer to his mother's in-
struction. She gazes at him with burning eyes of love. The
memory underlies a lewd parody of prayer, a remarkable passage of emotional range set off by subterranean passions. In a
ferocious mood after "the big scene of the sack" (36), his mate in
bliss, he considers praying, "prayer for prayer's sake when all
fails" (36). Yet prayer for what? Escape from the anguish of the
process? For love? The thought of himself on his knees triggers
the explosion. At the core of it lies withering mockery at the fa-
tuity of his praying—he was ever on his knees as the communal

spittoon—and mockery as well of Donne's holy sonnet, "Batter my heart, three person'd God."

"[S]een from behind on my knees arse bare on the summit of a muckheap" (36). He prays for respite, for sleep, to be released somewhere, elsewhere, "inconceivable" (37):

> aah no sound in the rectum a redhot spike that day we prayed no further/how often kneeling how often from behind kneeling from every angle from behind in every posture . . . / . . . farewell rats the ship is sunk a little less is all one begs/ . . . fire in the rectum how surmounted reflections on the passion of pain . . . / . . . the tins rattle like castanets and under me convulsed the mud goes guggle-guggle . . . / . . . had I only the little finger to raise to be wafted straight to Abraham's bosom I'd tell him to stick it up (37–38)

And from this display of despairing gaiety, as to say, fuck me God, murder me up the ass, answer my prayer, he shifts to vaunting egotism, the catechism of the artist: "understood everything and forgave nothing never could never disapproved anything really not even cruelty to animals never loved anything" (41).

Behind this venting is the suggestion that M in his former life destroyed himself in sodomy. The universal mud occasionally referred to as shit might seem Beckett's version of Dante's punishment for the sodomites. It might also seem that Beckett follows Dante's punishment for the sullen, who "guggle-guggle" under the mud of Styx. The mud certainly has these suggestive meanings. In the mete and rigorous artistry of Judgment, Dante is the supreme model. Beyond this, correspondences between *How It Is* and the *Inferno* do not play out, but are details of minor significance in a larger design.

Flawless justice has scripted M's blasphemous tirade to recur at that exact point in M's commentary on his journey. It is a feature of his torment: M reiterated ad nauseam, an infinitude of Ms murmuring to the mud, a quaqua (or caca) of voices, all reacting at that same moment to their transits as journeyers, all lifted out of the swill at that same instant. M ponders this. The same numberless Ms with the very same individualizing features, knowledgeable in mathematics, astronomy, physics, Latin, geography, history, the humanities in general, a polyglot, certainly fluent in more than one language, also evidently a writer —all writers. Everywhere himself replicated? Of course! He is completely egotistical and the judgment is that he has to live with his ego. It is a horrible cosmic joke that all he can produce is more Ms.

M, murmuring to the mud, sounds the full orchestral leitmotif of his hell by quoting the voice he locates externally:

> me we're talking of me without end . . . nothing [in Bom's possession]/then of a sudden like all that starts starts again [the journey] no knowing set forth forth again ten yards fifteen yards right leg right arm . . . a few images patches of blue [memories of his "life in the light"] a few words no sound cling to species [M's esprit with comb and hair dryer] a few sardines yawn of mud burst the sack drivel on drone on in a word the old road/from the next mortal to the next leading nowhere and saving correction no other goal than the next mortal cleave to him give him a name train him up bloody him all over with Roman capitals gorge on his fables [M's former life told by Pim] unite for life in stoic love to the last shrimp [shriek, Pim rosy warm and seeming dead] and a little longer/till the fine day when flip he vanishes leaving me his effects [his sack] and the sooth comes true the new life [part 3] no more journeys no more blue a murmur in the mud that's true all must be true and the other on his way ten yards fifteen yards what I for Pim Pim for me [a Pim, that is, named Bom]/all I hear hear no more . . . in my arms with my sack [the journey begins anew] (61–62)

The voice can only be a parody of the eternal voice of art, the mysterious creative spirit whom the artist addresses in his invocation—on his knees praying for the profound disquietude of creative possession. The interior life is a given; it is the hell of hells: mud, darkness, and terror. The recital aloud of his passing thoughts focuses him. Imagining a voice external to him as the source of his thoughts situates him—on his knees in prayer to the heavenly muse. If elected, he will live again in the act of producing another fiction. The voice is separate from the conscious intelligence of the artist, who is the steward, the facilitator who brings a measure of that genius into being. He hears it only imperfectly and there is no telling when he will no longer hear it,

no longer sense the coming of the stranger when, hovering between being and nothingness, the self dissolves into its new creation and crosses the threshold of the renewed artistic process.
The end of the novel portrays the artist when he is no longer
alive to his muse, in the grasp of terror, which is the stimulus for
his faith in the externality of the voice. Throughout the creative
process, he is a suppliant.

The scheme then is boldly, sensuously set forth. The narration is from the inside, the narrator on his narration, speculating and probing, what is this place? Is there an end? "[I]s it
possible the old business of grace in this sewer why want us all
alike" (61). He flatly lies in order to find contradictions in the
flawless conception. Finding himself out strengthens his faith in
it. Pim, he says, is two or three inches shorter than he. If so, why
imagine torturing him for confirmation that he, M, exists, that
Pim is not a copy of him? He trains Pim, instrumentalizes him
to speak of his, M's, life, impelled by the justice of the place to
deny his own existence, the chance for companionship, Pim as
confirmation that M is there still. Of course, doubt of that engenders the fiction. The writer only exists through his creations,
the artist being of all people the least sure of his own existence.

M enters stage two "clawing for the take" (48). He tortures
Pim to bring alive the raw material of his writing. The novel is
the story of what is involved in creation. Pim instrumentalized
speaks M's life (in the sense that M relives his life through the
mistreatment of Pim) just as M degrades himself in order to
speak Bom's life when crossing over the threshold to a new creation. Every new story is born of the same torture. For the flawless justice of the place, the artistry of his own retributive
justice, impels M, devoid of memory and incapable of speech, to
possess his victim—possibly to accentuate the sadistic urgency
of the writer as vampire.

All of this is served up quite graphically by the *conoscente*,
who can do nothing otherwise in the service of his art but position himself along Pim's left side, his shoulder overlapping
Pim's, who lies in the mud, arse up, arms extended, his face
turned to the left, his sack clutched in his left hand. At one point
M takes control of the sack, removes the can-opener, placing it
for easy access between Pim's thighs, and returns the sack to

Pim's grasp, but with his own fingers, with their unspeakable nails, snuggled between Pim's fingers. M's right arm moves freely in an arc from above Pim's head to below his buttocks, and has leverage from the elevation of his body over Pim's.

He describes Pim's training with shameless pleasure. He has no inhibiting reflex. Being for him is not holding himself at a distance. Experience has meaning only to the extent that it serves his art.

Training commences on the momentous discovery that Pim has a voice. He sings, warbling a few words: "first lesson theme song I dig my nails into his armpit right hand right pit he cries I withdraw them thump with fist on skull his face sinks in the mud his cries cease end of first lesson" (62).

After repeated pummelings, Pim learns to sing on command, to stop on command; louder, thump on right kidney; softer, finger in the anus. With the can-opener M scores Pim's back and jabs the point into his buttocks. Trial and error, stab and thump, extort from Pim a brief murmur instead of a howl. Exactions of countless thumps on his kidney, murmur louder, louder, extort a halting speech, "hey you me what don't" (68). M claps Pim's buttocks signifying "bravo" (105), and begins phase two, training Pim to recognize and reply to words which he cuts into Pim's back with his nails in capital letters. Pim is taught to speak of M's life, "little scenes the curtains parted the mud parted the light went on he saw for me" (73).

Pim begins to speak of M's wife. M punches his face in the mud. Pim goes on, memories of diminished passion, "tried to revive it through the arse too late she fell from the window or jumped broken solemn/in the ward before she went every day all winter she forgave me everybody" (77). The memory repeats, in variations of the same details, the hospital room, the mistletoe he could not find for her, views from the window, and abruptly, as if in a leap from the hospital room, images of dereliction, "always a hole a ruin always a crust" (78). M provides no commentary. Connective phrases and flashes of signal words transmit the story, the memories he is reliving. A motif of broken backs becomes part of the sequence, his father's from a collapsed scaffolding, his dog's from the wheels of a cart. The implicit links in the sequences of memories are always the same, from the failed efforts to resuscitate passion to her jump from the window, lingering death, forgiveness, his bringing flowers, and the abandonment of himself to be used and shat on: "from hell to home hell to home to hell" (79), flotsam among the detritus. These events will always be at the heart of the fiction he creates.

Aspects of the composition underscore his own martyrdom in the service of art, in producing works that may even have a redeeming value. The text's division by three, before, with, and after Pim; mention of God thirty-three times, evoking Christ's sacrifice;[21] and reference to the crucifixion in arms spread in the form of a cross and Roman capitals cut in "miraculous flesh" (51); and possibly even Krim and Kram (his biographers) as his apostles. The process is one of martyring and being martyred, always the same, the same sickening goads to produce the recital, the same fading out of the victim, the same hopeless urgency for love, and the same nadir point of terror.

"[S]omething wrong there" (25) is a telling refrain. M's drive for some kind of human validation is at odds with the demands of his art. "[C]ut thrust DO YOU LOVE ME" (75), drilling deeper, craving companionship:

> if he loved me a little if Pim loved me a little yes or no if I loved him a little in the dark the mud in spite of all a little affection find someone at last someone find you at last live together glued together love each other a little love a little without being loved be loved a little without loving answer that (74)

It is a question meant to underscore the sacrifice. A jute sack with food in tins must do as blissful other.

M wonders if Pim, the countless repetitions of being with Pim, is a chance for working out an expiation, "prayer without words against a stable-door long icy toil towards the too late all-forgiving" (91). Or Pim for "hanging on to humankind" (94), or "just a drop of ditch-water I'd be glad of a sup at this hour" (91). He cleaves to him for "always" (95), even if Pim be a corpse and replicated a millionfold. If only he could refute, escape the suspicion that "no Pim . . . / . . . not Pim I who murmur all that" (87), or bury his face in the mud and remain mum until time ends and maybe he too will end. "HERE HERE" (96), he imagines cutting Pim to the bone, smashing his face in the mud, demanding Pim to speak of his own life, but Pim can only whisper bits and pieces of M's life. Pim is M's creation.

"[S]omething wrong there" may also be a reminder that in the postmodernist works of Beckett objective unity is an illusion and the critics' efforts to display coherent artistic form are deadening falsifications. Beckett argues this (it is worth repeating) in his writings about art, claiming that a new art form is needed, one which of necessity must always be a failure both as objective representation and as subjective expression. Art can only represent the instability of the subject and the indeterminacy of the object. The artist moreover is torn by a need to disparage his desire for order and structure and to disrupt it altogether. The artist either strives for the new or is an antiquarian.[22]

Yet I continue to discover that coherence, and the vividness of story, are foregrounded by the very devices presumably intended to block meaning. Perhaps it is simply that construing meaning is necessary for survival. The impulse cannot be disarmed, only frustrated. However confusing the initial impression of *How It Is*, its effect will be like that of a Rorschach blot, "a concatenation of possibilities" that the mind will endow with meaning.[23] It usually comes by way of trial and error, the eureka of a powerful impression that gathers meaning to it and radiates continuously from that center. The proliferation of theoretical thinking about art may have been spurred by the critics' efforts to keep up with the experimental, though in doing so, a gap has greatly widened between the critics and the vast majority of working writers who are not experimenting like Beckett and are repelled by the critics' praxis. Many of Beckett's strongest admirers regard him as a writer-philosopher, at least half philosopher, concerned in his art with the problem of the perceiving mind and its self-perception, definitions of the self, identity's definitive borders, the endless recedings of origins and authorship, examining his art in relationship to the speculative inquiries of philosophy. He is linked to Descartes, Geulincx, Malebranche, Wittgenstein, Heidegger, Derrida, Levinas, Kierkegaard, Ortega y Gasset, Sartre, Leibniz, and others. But this is essentially, it seems to me, pointing out how Beckett garnishes the entrée.

To summarize: the novel enacts the creative process, the story behind the story, stepping into the process at the point in part 3—the very end of the novel—when the writer is without inspiration, no longer knows he exists, and prays to the muse a repetitive quasi-magical incantation. He wishes to be possessed by memory in order to create. Then, in part 4, he searches for the new work's point of departure, the writer's consciousness caught in a no-man's-land between the discarded and the not yet imagined. Bom is the stranger through whom and of whom the writer speaks, reenacting the past and feeling his way into the new fiction. Then in part 1, the journey begins, shared as from a spy-hole, with the observer participating, seeking a conception, sorting his memories; experimenting with voice, emotional boundaries, a stance; discerning the minimal necessary effects; discovering the laws of the fiction. In part 2 comes the instrumentalizing of Pim to sing in M's voice and the violation and sacrifice of everyone and everything to the story. Finally in part 3, the last stage of composition (before the prayer for inspiration and welcoming plunge into the usurpation of a new stranger): M examines the conception, seeks ways of opening it out, hits on a transformative vision, and finds the closure.

That transformative insight comes by way of spatial perspectives, diagrams of M's hell, which expand the conception from the "how it is" of the creative process to the all-inclusive "how it is" of being—life as Holocaust. The artist discovers humanity in himself and bears the tale.

Couples form again and again along an immense circuit each time for the first time, two strangers uniting in the interest of torment: a thousand, a million, an infinite number of couples, conscious and responsive for brief instants at a time, then gone from each other for vast tracks of time, thankful for the crumb, the cry, the paltry conscious moments of pain; "all is not dead one drinks one gives to drink goodbye" (122). Or, altogether they resemble a great inchworm moving by the jerks and spasms of an impulsion to become torturers in order to be. In this endless caravan which moves forward when M escapes Bom, when Pim escapes M, when Bem escapes Pim, when the next in line escapes Bem, and the next escapes his torturer impelled forward to the

next in line, must there be a stimulus every time at the beginning of the line initiating the transmission to be a torturer? Or is
the impulse innate? The question boils down to whether or not
life as torture and suffering is self-perpetuating or a hands-on
affair, which might imply a surprise to come. Fancy "days of
great gaiety" (108), everyone on the move through the shit like
the "scissiparous frenzy" (113) of latrinal slime worms, a peri-
staltic forward motion like turds in the bowels to be "shat into
the open air" (124).

M perceives the ugly generative force of that endless proces-
sion, the human pageant. He imagines the couples coalescing
into an agglutination, an "immeasurable wallow" (141) of flesh
inching eastward, propelled by the collective victims' stronger
urge to move on—overcoming the collective torturers' desire to
hold them fast—a moving on, to be sure, toward the prospect of
enjoyment.

M finally imagines not a million beings but four, like beetles
on an oval track biting and being bitten from behind. M knows
only those in front and behind him. If he is B, he never encounters D, just as C never encounters A. The diagram leads him to
the speculation of knowledge by repute, passing from torturer to
victim. A tells B of his torturer D. If perceived as a line of a million beings, a closed curve, everyone ahead and behind B would
know of his existence by dint of Roman capitals. Nothing is
gainsaid by these speculations—possibly the experiment with
"callers" (12) in part 1.

He fancies there are not four beings but three, each sand-
wiched between a torturer and a victim. This means an agglutination, a nasty ball turning clockwise and inching eastward like
a wheel. The three may as well be pictured as one, just as two
preying on each other may as well be one. In any one part is contained the whole human pageant, impelled to sting itself if there
is no one ahead of it in line to sting.

These depths, then, out of which art is created have nothing
to do with healing, comforting, befriending; with insight and
reintegration; with reaching out as an act of sacred passion. This
art rises from a mass grave bearing witness to the absence of redemption, to the ostentation of self-elegies, to the hypocrisy of

late reckonings, an art fitting for "an age/when man became so debased/that he killed on his own, with lust, not just on orders."[24]

Art cannot stop the process of torture. The witness can change nothing. He may as well be murmuring to the mud. Alone in the muck, he discerns and bears the tale, the story behind the story of "life in the light." He tortures himself because there is no one else to torture, to know by the pain that he still exists, and he prays for inspiration in an incantatory invocation to the muse, begging to be taken on again as torturer and servant.

How It Is, a new, transformative version of the writer's torment of ambivalence, may have been inspired by Kafka's "In the Penal Colony." Kafka wrote it in three days, inspired by an emissary from Felice Bauer, his former fiancée, asking for reconciliation and rousing him from peaceful numbness. The relationship was in its second of five years (1912–17) during which Kafka wrote her over five hundred letters. When she withdrew, he flirted with suicide; marriage would be his bond to community. When she threatened to take his epistolary ardor at its word, he felt like a man before a firing squad; he begged Felice to accept his self-accusations and reject him. The resumption of the torture of ambivalence—to live in the world or to dwell in the cellar of the imagination—gave rise to his fantasy of vengeance and self-destruction.

An officer in charge of an obsolete system of justice explains the precise mechanism of a torture machine, commenting adoringly on its function and with aesthetic appreciation on the victim's every convulsion. The story is the perfect wish-fulfillment of power, of imposing one's will on another without any limits. The officer's submission to and destruction by the machine gone haywire is not definitive. The world of the old Commandant hovers somewhere in the future, awaiting the time for its return in an inexorable cycle.

In the murk of the story's private symbolism, Kafka atones for torturing Felice through sacrificing the officer to the machine; torture and judgment follow in a continuous cycle. "*Dig deeper*, mon ami."[25] *How It Is* depicts the imagination at work in the hell from which it takes flight on the wings of torture. A key to Beckett's advance from *Texts for Nothing* to *How It Is* is the discovery of the importance of torture to the imagination. *Endgame* can be seen as a step in the direction of this discovery, where Hamm is the author's imagination personified, and the stage set is a skull-like rotunda with Hamm surviving by torturing Clov.

8

The Lost Ones

Beckett worked on *The Lost Ones* in 1965 and 1966, and then after a break of four years completed it in 1970, writing the fifteenth of the fifteen paragraphs. The critical response is baffling. James Knowlson and John Pilling (1980), speaking of the hint in the last sentence that the victims of the hideous world of the cylinder will come to life again, all rekindle again, observe that this world will "thus once again become a place of systematic polity teetering on the edge of anarchy."[26] To them, *The Lost Ones* "resembles a deeply considered, and admirably restrained, exploration of *terra incognita.*"[27] They hear in the voice of narration "a desperate quality about these weighty sentences that suggests Beckett is feeling the strain of keeping up the Olympian calm that has marked his enterprise from the beginning."[28] This strain on Beckett can also be detected in the occasional "wryness of tone,"[29] though, on the whole, they find the voice "pedantically dry and remote,"[30] and "[t]he glazed surface of the prose" impenetrable to "what lies behind the impassive detachment of the speaker."[31] Ruby Cohn (2001) refers to the narrator's naïveté, insensitivity, and dryness of tone in tension with the theatricality of the piece, of the inadequacy of the speaker to deal with the complexities of "a Dante-nourished imagination," and of "a cruelly gripping account of a social system that is at once self-enclosed and parallel to those we know."[32]

I belabor these remarks to underscore my bafflement over the readings of these most established of Beckett's critics, written as if they share some secret that Beckett told them, a prohibition against speaking of an obvious source of the piece. In this chapter, I use a parallel reading of *The Lost Ones* and Kafka's "In the Penal Colony" to open Beckett's story to examination from a variety of perspectives.

"'It's a remarkable piece of apparatus,' said the officer to the explorer" in Kafka's "In the Penal Colony."[33] Ditto for the circular apparatus of *The Lost Ones:* "fifty metres round and sixteen high for the sake of harmony."[34] The preview to the exhibit guilefully echoes Dante: "Abode where lost bodies roam each searching for its lost one. Vast enough for search to be in vain. Narrow enough for flight to be in vain" (202). In all are some two hundred naked people, of both sexes and all ages, though few children, most in feverish motion. This apparatus has, so to say, an observation deck from which a spokesman conveys its aspects to us, the visitor-explorer. The composition is rubber-like, twelve million centimeters of total surface, one body per square meter. Every detail in the material structure of the apparatus has its significance—size, light, climate, niches, ladders, rubber-like surface (allowing those braining themselves only brief moments of unconsciousness). The interpreter points out three precise zones of activity and four types of victims. Eventually, the toy will run down, entropy is the law, but with so "fluctuant" (206) a slowness that those numbering in the fourth category, "the vanquished," will increase imperceptibly. Lying down is prohibited. The cylinder being young, there are only five "vanquished" sitting against the wall with heads bowed "in the attitude which wrung from Dante one of his rare wan smiles" (205). The smile is rather on the lips of our interpreter making an erudite joke, playing a little Bach. The allusion is to Belacqua's laziness in *Purgatorio,* Canto IV, line 122, which moves Dante's "lips into a little smile."[35] But the interpreter knows that all in the cylinder reside in Hell. Dante's smile on the lips of the interpreter amounts to a joke at the expense of "the vanquished," as if they are merely lazy, and a sneer at the rest, who do not yet get it.

The doom, of course, is absolute. Entombed in a cylinder, hermetically sealed, where light pulses feverishly, a rapidly flickering yellow murk that burns out the eyes, blindness ensured, "the vanquished" are prematurely blind, and where the temperature is no less artful, oscillating every four seconds between twenty-five degrees centigrade and five degrees centigrade, desiccating the skin, especially the mucous membranes, and accentuating the pain of contact. This is impossible to avoid, particularly in the central arena, the first of the three zones, where the searching throng is in ceaseless motion and the sound of contact like the swarm of insects. Also there are the dull thuds of fists against breasts in sudden fury.

"[T]he notion is abroad that there exists a way out," sneers the interpreter, and notes the two schools of thought on this question—that of a secret tunnel, and that of a trap door in the ceiling, both ways "to nature's sanctuaries." He smiles, how they "give [themselves] the lie" (206). To perceive what goes for thinking among these people, "one must be in the secret of the gods." Yes, this glimmer of hope, this "fatuous little light will be assuredly the last to leave them always assuming they are darkward bound"—if not already dead. "An instant of fraternity" would suffice to disprove their trap door theory, "[b]ut outside their explosions of violence this sentiment is as foreign to them as to butterflies." And then the spokesperson proffers an insight: they are stupid people, "not so much to want of heart or intelligence as to the ideal preying on one and all" (tapping the ash of his cigarette), namely, docility before the law, which forbids them to search there. "So much for this inviolable zenith [the forbidden ceiling] where for amateurs of myth lies hidden a way out to earth and sky" (207). Witty, calling the hapless condemned "amateurs of myth" because they relish a hope about which they do nothing but dream.

This sneering and sarcasm are characteristic of the narration, though when the details of the cylinder are not demonstrably linked to the ingeniousness of the apparatus, its "harmony," or to surmises about the behavior of its victims, the narrator seems as matter-of-fact as the officer in "In the Penal Colony"—an adoring matter-of-factness:

> Now just have a look at this machine. . . . Up till now a few things still had to be set by hand. . . . Won't you take a seat? . . . its one drawback is that it gets so messy. . . . Getting the needles fixed in the glass was a technical problem. . . . now anyone can look through the glass and watch the inscription taking form on the body. . . . it's not supposed to kill a man straight off, but only after

an interval of, on an average, twelve hours; the turning point is reckoned to come at the sixth hour. . . . So it keeps on writing deeper and deeper. . . . After two hours the felt gag is taken away, for he has no longer strength to scream. . . . some warm rice pap is poured, from which . . . his tongue can lap. Not one of them ever misses the chance. . . . Only about the sixth hour does the man lose all desire to eat. I usually kneel down here at that moment and observe what happens. . . . Enlightenment comes to the most dull-witted. . . . [It] might tempt one to get under the Harrow one-self. . . . the man begins to understand the inscription. . . . often enough I would be squatting there with a small child in either arm. How we all absorbed the look of transfiguration on the face of the sufferer, how we bathed our cheeks in the radiance of that justice, achieved at last and fading so quickly! What times these were, my comrade! ("In the Penal Colony," 141–54)

In a manner very reminiscent of this, we—explorer-visitor—learn of the modes of activity in the cylinder, and of the laws become instinct insuring against pandemonium.

All are searchers. "For the passion to search is such that no place may be left unsearched" (219). This need promotes circulation, this impetus to seek continuously—those thronging in the central arena—for faces. Many would know each other; relatives, friends, acquaintances are many, but difficult to make out by the half-blind in "the press and gloom." "Man and wife are strangers two paces apart" (213). Should they be close enough to touch and exchange a look, they continue on without sign of recognition. "Whatever it is they are searching for it is not that" (213), while along the periphery the searching is less hapless, less agitated.

In all there are fifteen ladders of different sizes for the two hundred odd victims along the wall. Laws obtain to their use, and for the conduct of those waiting in queue, and for passage from the arena to this inner zone, which grows cluttered by the occasional bodies of "the vanquished," and by a class of victims, the "sedentary searchers," who are respected as "semi-sages" (210). Climbing makes free, yet these squatters go berserk when accidentally bumped by a ladder queue and forced to move. The need to climb is not altogether dead in them, but "subject to strange resurrections" (204–205). Ditto for "the vanquished;" on occasion they revive and "start to search afresh as famished as the unthinkable first day." Even so, time moves in their direction, slowly: as "a great heap of sand sheltered from the wind lessened by three grains every second year and every following increased by two" (212) steadily disperses.

Climbers are free to select one of six vacant apertures, there being twenty, which extend around the cylinder above a certain point in the wall. All of these apertures, or niches, provide a place to be apart. Some openings extend into dead-end tunnels; others lead to connecting tunnels. Yet it all betokens hapless searching; the overriding imperative, like an instinct, is all there is—the search for a face, an opening, to be moving—an incomprehensible striving like panic, and though mindless—"None looks within himself where none can be" (211)—yet feeling "the incessant [strain]" of "moral distress" (214). All is feverish motion and agitation of moral distress without interior thought, until irregular sudden suspension, when everything stops—the flickering, the oscillation, the swarm, the hum—everyone rigid in attitude, as if all were part of a mechanism pushed into pause (the better to see you with, my dears), ten seconds of terror—to "answer the needs of the cylinder. So all is for the best" (215–16)—after which everything boots up again.

Of course "for the best." It is the place of "certitudes" (216), observes the Commandant's spokesman. One might take pictures during these programmed moments of interruption; for while erection is rare in the cylinder, it occurs. "[H]appy penetration in the nearest tube" seems the rule. "The spectacle then is one to be remembered of frenzies prolonged in pain and hopelessness long beyond what even the most gifted lovers can achieve in camera." Caught in one of the "lulls," the sight of such lovemaking can quite "[verge] . . . on the obscene" (220). True enough, the machine degrades, and its adherents sneer, but of all remarkable aspects of life in the cylinder, it should be these aghast fornicators who give our informant a hard-on.

As for "certitudes," the speaker cannot explain one glaring circumstance. In passing from the arena to the zone of climbers, searchers must wait, rotating in Indian file along its border, for the cue to enter. Entry is determined by an opening in the fixed number within that inner circle. What conceivable rule of priority prevents a state of anarchy—"saturation of the intermediate zone" and fury and violence in a stampede for the ladders? To this our informant replies, "the answers are clear and easy to give. It only remains to dare." Aha, a flaw in the mechanism and bravura for answer. Or, "All has not been told and never shall be" (219), implying unspeakable obscenities, though what, we can't imagine, could remain concealed?

In this scenography, then, no cattle cars, crematoria, factories, no lethal gas, or I. G. Farben, no SS, or thirty-eight camps attached to the main Auschwitz camp, no *Arbeit Macht Frei,* no "death begins with the shoes," or parades, or striped rags, or tattoos, or ersatz coffee, or cutaneous edemas, no boils, leg ulcers, abcesses, suppurating sores, no dysentery, no roll calls. Yet that world is called into being by the cylinder, and by its adherent and spokesman, who probably is not a monster, or idiot, or pervert. He is a functionary of the state, more pedant than brute, perhaps. From the observation deck, frenzied seeking, brainings with the rungs of a ladder, the berserk violence of disturbed squatters, a queue falling upon an unauthorized seeker, fists and skulls dashed against the walls, frenzied intercourse, the inspecting of faces and bodies and thumbing open of eyes, a swarm sound as of insects, a "faint stridulence" (223) of the persistent twofold vibration, the frozen moments of cessation. The cylinder world cannot be separated from the history of fascism in Europe. Visitor, you are not a stranger.

"So on infinitely," begins the last paragraph, which Beckett wrote four years after the first, "until towards the unthinkable end if this notion is maintained a last body of all by feeble fits and starts is searching still" (222). This last one of all gropes his way to the first of "the vanquished," a woman who, because of her rootedness, had become a point of reference known as "north" (221). He sweeps back her long hair, raises her head, and gently with his thumbs opens her blank eyes. The whole action has about it the feel of a tableau, the last paying tribute to the first. But more likely, that is simply the way the machine works, his kneeling before her and searching "those calm wastes" (223), then closing his own eyes and dropping her head. He pauses, it is the final whirring of the machine, "finds at last his place and pose whereupon dark descends and . . . the temperature comes to rest not far from freezing point." It is the end. "So much roughly speaking for the last state of the cylinder and of this little people of searchers one first of whom if a man in some unthinkable past for the first time bowed his head if this notion is maintained" (223). The hint of the circularity of form lies in the darkness coming down like a curtain in a play as the performers freeze in position. So perhaps it is not altogether the end, roughly speaking.

In Kafka, the idea of a repeat performance, the apparatus restored and refreshed, is implanted at the teahouse, the meeting place for adherents of the old Commandant and site of his grave, where the explorer pauses in flight from the penal colony. "[H]e felt the power of past days" (166). He kneels before the stone, uncovered for him from beneath a table, and recites the prophecy: "the Commandant will rise again. . . . Have faith and wait!" (167). Perhaps a forecast of the later "harmony" of the Third Reich?

"[H]ey, something wrong there" (375), says the Unnamable about his own exaggerations. Similarly, my implicating the reader's conscience may seem false to the spirit of Beckett, who more likely intends to nullify appeals to conscience. Thus, the cylinder world also might suggest the next step back before human life: people seen as some lower life form that is only distinguished by its numbers—no will, no consciousness—a blind and furious searching, drying up and dying, in a hostile environment, without connection—like sperm. It is our prehistory: the ugliness of human life at its foundation, the chance and fragile nature of life continuing—of there being a tunnel that is not dead-end—a fatal warrant for continuing. "And finally, to wind up with, song and dance of thanksgiving by victim, to celebrate his nativity" (*The Unnamable* 352). The cylinder world recalls the Unnamable's flamboyant hatred and execration of human life that is the occasion for his Worm story—those passages of prolonged bitterness in the novel-long "no" to existence.

And possibly the cylinder world is a place set apart for artists, where the writer imaginatively dead still goes through the motions—seeking faces, looking into the eyes of "the vanquished," climbing ladders, crawling into dead-end tunnels, refusing to go on, violent when disturbed, given to strange resurrections, vibrating to two storms, dazedly searching, in frenzies of despair, loving nobody, in mental and physical agony, dashing head against the wall for brief moments of unconsciousness, coupling for the hell of it, going blind, going on.

One further take seems possible. See the author looking down on life, leaning on his elbows. He is fascinated—no, disgusted, contemptuous, and mildly curious, thinly smiling and wondering at his patience, just as Milton's God would were He to have been confronted with what his creation had become. No point asking such theological questions (because redemption and regeneration are impossible in Beckett's world) as "Who's to blame? Who's responsible for this repulsive toy?" Perhaps Beckett needed a Nazi mouthpiece to tell the truth about the world as he saw it. That truth roused him from the paralysis he describes in *Texts for Nothing.* In *Texts,* writing is a process fueled by a torturous ambivalence between hopeless choices that inevitably lead to the extinguishing of the imagination. In *The Lost Ones,* interest in the world is revivified by the discovery that the species itself is defined by its lust for both torture and escape.

9

Beckett and Kafka

1

Kafka is an analogue for Beckett, a source, a model, someone to react against, even a forebear in the sense that Borges speaks of Kafka as a chosen precursor. "The Metamorphosis" stands like a silent witness behind the *Nouvelles* (the four stories Beckett wrote in 1946). Behind the trilogy looms *The Castle*. The epic poem embedded in *The Unnamable*, of a hero fighting for some remnant of self against the loss of identity in a world inimical to the sacred, is also the story of *The Castle*. I go further, making the case for *The Castle*'s importance to the genesis of the trilogy (1947 to January 1950), for it enabled Beckett to imagine Molloy and his strategies for survival, Malone's martyrdom, and the Unnamable's lucidity.

The issue for me is not only Beckett's indebtedness but also the depth of my own engagement; Kafka helps me find my bearings in Beckett. I get at the story—that which is central—and the purpose of the rest—the artistry.

Texts for Nothing (1951) might as well be dedicated to Kafka. The landscapes of the sequence are dreamscapes; the torment driving the sequence is the Kafkaesque tension between world and imagination; and Beckett's nihilism about the worth of art is also Kafkaesque. Kafka's ape in "A Report to an Academy" stands behind Hamm in *Endgame* (1956), or, perhaps, helps illuminate Hamm in his struggle against annihilation. *How It Is* (1961) is surely Beckett's most Kafkaesque text in its poetics. The narrative, treated realistically, is a grotesque symbolic allegory about the creative process, inspiration, and ultimately hu-

man nature. *Imagination Dead Imagine* (1965), which describes
a torture chamber and the violent satisfactions of torture, invites the reader's participation even more directly than Kafka's
officer in "In the Penal Colony," which probably was in Beckett's
mind when he wrote the story. Similarly, any discussion of *The
Lost Ones* (1970) should consider a parallel reading with "In the
Penal Colony."

In this final chapter I discuss what Beckett learned from
Kafka in two main ways—by showing the importance of *The
Castle* to Beckett's stance and method in the trilogy; and by
evoking the Kafka we imagine from his diaries and letters and
from the man portrayed by his biographers, contending that
Kafka the literary figure helped Beckett envisage Molloy and
Malone and make the transition from the *Nouvelles* to the tril-
ogy.

2

The third, most difficult, least read, novel of the trilogy
stands at the summit of Beckett's writings. Who is the Unnamable? The Unnamable is a voice that cannot stop speaking. Perhaps it is the voice of an isolated consciousness. Perhaps he
exists as thought, thought that he hears as if it were from an external voice. He cannot be sure that it is his voice, or another's,
or others'. Has he an existence, a self-identity, an "I"? How can
he know? He's in darkness, immobilized, speaking, if it is he
speaking. Somehow he knows about human life, which he
loathes and fears as a punishment more dreadful than his desperate plight. He tells stories about characters who cannot abide
life, hapless outcasts, others who have devised strategies for survival, in order to verify his existence. After all, somebody is
making up his stories. But can he be sure that that somebody is
he and not another, or others who impute a voice and a self to
him? He cannot prove that he is not their invention. His own literary characters may be their recruits, helping in the process of
extinguishing his being by coaxing him into assuming the form
they have invented for him. He cannot prove himself the inventor rather than the invented, even if he went on proliferating an
infinite number of inexpugnable antiheroes like Mahood, who

might seem to make a mockery of the idea of the Unnamable's characters being henchmen in his conscription.

The powerful notion that he is being punished for resisting his birth into life provides ever-renewing material for speculation—about where he is, what is being done to him, and by whom. Despite self-ridicule, he cannot stop embellishing the story. He speculates he is being tested. A supreme power, his master, requires something from him. Praise is it, intoned, in order to obtain forgiveness? Obedience to the will of the master's henchmen? His capacity to believe in his situation continuously surprises him; he believes with bitter earnestness in the fiction of his persecution: his being glutted on lies—reared for the great confounding, life. But perhaps the good master will reward him for holding out when convinced at last that the Unnamable will never allow himself to be born.

The idea of birth inspires his story of Worm's nativity. Parodic, defiant, he loses himself in the depiction of what it means to be wakened into sentience, given bodily awareness, organs of sense, a brain—life, the vilest of tortures. They cannot co-opt him; he will never serve. They will never violate him as they do Worm! Flamboyant hatred strengthens his conviction in the story of his persecution—for the moment, moment to moment. So he keeps at bay doubts about his existence.

If only he could stop the voice. If silence was possible, so perhaps would self-presence be possible. Against the other or others who would foist on him a counterfeit, human identity, he "stops" the voice, turns it against itself by negating every utterance, empties it of meaning by reducing it to sounds of rhythmic breathing, in quest of a nonverbal core to himself—of a trace of himself, if not the discovery of his "I am." Despairing, an "it" trying to find a self in silence as it tried in speech, he quickens the pace, as if he might find the door to self by racing into a jabber bordering on incoherence, into nonsense. He knows the quest to be unattainable, cannot relinquish it, brings to its service the fairy tale of the good master who at any time can reward his exploit by releasing him to himself; and so, in quest of this key to himself through silence, he swings back to the opposite pole of fictional projections and endless exegesis. Can he escape? Is that why he tells stories? Does he escape in his stories? Why must he tell stories? Is he speaking or listening? If stuffed with their words like a parrot, how can he do other than proclaim himself one of them? Why do they take into their heads that he had better exist? What is he guilty of? How many are in the same boat? Who is in charge? What does the master want?

Fictions, speculations, building and rebuilding the edifice of his persecutions, are futile. He can never prove that he exists. Dissolution is not an alternative. He must go on. When in a panic of dissolution he speaks to erase what he speaks, and we respond with pained empathy to the frantic blither, something other than a maniacal language game (and the issues it raises in contemporary theories of language and subjectivity) grips our interest.[1] We believe in the story of the Unnamable's resistance to persecution, and feel the exaltation of witnessing a strange justice—the struggle for the impossibility of justice to which the alternative is spiritual death. The Unnamable is the new figure of epic grandeur for the age of Kafka and the death camps.

3

The linkage between Beckett's *Watt* (written 1942, published 1953) and Kafka's *The Castle* (written 1922, published 1926) has been obvious to a number of commentators.[2] Ruby Cohn (1961), in the most detailed comparison of the two novels, questions whether *Watt* could have been written without the example of *The Castle*. She says that "Kafka's almost incredible feat has been to base our compassion on our doubt."[3] In other words, we feel for K. because truth is inaccessible, which makes his quest hopeless; in his world there is no truth, only different and contradictory perspectives. There is temporal coherence and causality; the portrayal is, to use Kafka's words, "full-bodied," but at the same time, it is fantastic, senseless, "a dream, a dim hovering."[4] Beckett's narrator, Sam, in *Watt*, describes the fabric of the world of his hero in the same way. "[A] thing that was nothing had happened, with the utmost formal distinctness."[5] The problem of interpretation for Watt (named for the interrogative pronoun) as for K. and the reader is "in foisting a meaning there where no meaning appeared" (*Watt* 77).

Such worlds as one finds in Kafka and Beckett make omniscience impossible. Both authors are obliged to present truth through a first-person consciousness, and both heroes must, says Cohn, "fail, finally, to reach their goals—and never understand the cause of their failure, or even the nature of their compulsive quests."[6] She calls the two heroes "victims of . . . uncertainty" and their fates "bitter ends"—ends which neither can anticipate.[7]

I find Cohn's remarks no less true for a comparison of *The Castle* with *The Unnamable*; true, and yet false—false to the reader's identification with, and loyalty to, the heroes. The moral ground becomes surer, the allegiance to each hero firmer, when one reads Kafka through Beckett and vice versa.

Hans H. Hiebel (1997) says that Beckett's stance toward the world is that of the anthropologist, and that he is like Kafka in this respect. Both writers "isolate certain aspects of reality and work with reduction, concentration and abstraction," exhibiting human traits in the essential, and doing so with humor.[8] We are found burying ourselves alive for security ("The Burrow"); communicating with meaningless whistles ("Josephine the Singer, or the Mouse Folk"); producing no more than an endless repetition of thought ("Play"); existing in a never ending, monotonous life pattern ("Quadrat"); driven by compulsion, unaware of one another, blind and imprisoned in the eternal circle of come and go (*The Lost Ones*); lying to ourselves about help from heaven ("Investigations of a Dog"). Hiebel's remarks (like Cohn's) are true as general observations about the artistry of Beckett and Kafka.[9] But even more salient for the student of Beckett is to think of the world of Kafka as source for Beckett's anthropological investigations, and the trilogy as his findings.

4

He would wish, as a writer, Kafka said, to be able to portray "life, while still retaining its natural full-bodied rise and fall," and "simultaneously" show it "no less clearly as a nothing, a dream, a dim hovering." Imagine, he said, "hammer[ing] together a table with painful and methodical technical efficiency, and simultaneously do nothing at all," that is, make the hammering "still bolder, still surer, still more real and, if you will, still more senseless." Part of him disclaimed that notion. Such writing could only be "a vindication of nothingness, a justification of non-entity, a touch of animation which he wanted to lend to non-entity." Still, he was attracted to the idea, "a sort of farewell that he took from the illusive world of youth; although youth had never directly deceived him, but only caused him to be deceived by the utterances of all the authorities he had around him."[10]

Did not Kafka achieve this effect in *The Castle*? Is not K. caught in a life-and-death struggle that is at the same time a senseless pantomime? The description also fits Beckett's *The Unnamable*. In *The Unnamable* there is more furious consternation in the senseless hammering, as if K. had become the Unnamable after ages of the pantomime and was undergoing it again in protest and refusal. Kafka well understood the tease enabling the quest to go on, calling it, ironically, "a vestige of faith," a belief that change, release is possible, that during the struggle "the Master may chance to walk along the corridor, contemplate the prisoner, and say: 'You must not lock up this one again. He is to come to me'" (*Great Wall* 281). This is the pipe dream of salvation that keeps the Unnamable going.

Close to the ongoing end of K.'s story, he is summoned at four in the morning by the high secretary of an official at the Herrenhof Inn, the establishment reserved for Castle officials and their business. K. enters the wrong door literally reeling from exhaustion. A wrinkled, glittering-eyed, pixieish man, "rubb[ing] his hands in involuntary merriment" at the surprise visit, introduces himself as "the strongest liaison" between the Castle and village secretaries.[11] His name is Bürgel. Instantly he shows a keen interest in K. and prepares to take notes. "[P]ay attention," he says, "there are sometimes, after all, opportunities," lucky chances by which "more can be achieved than by means of life-long exhausting efforts" (337). And he adds philosophically, eying K., who is already half asleep, "But then again, of course, these opportunities are in accord with the general situation in so far as they are never made use of" (337–38). Lo, the genie from the lamp, the fairy-tale loophole, providing entry to the

Castle at precisely the moment for K. when he is too exhausted to make use of it.

Bürgel proceeds to a disquisition on the variety of ways secretaries frustrate and demoralize applicants, especially applicants summoned to night interrogations when the secretaries are tired and must safeguard themselves against appeals to pity. Incaution "positively tears the official organization to shreds" (348). Nevertheless—however—wake up, K.! The rare great opportunities exist when the applicant quite literally has to do nothing but stumble in and "put forward his plea, for which fulfillment is already waiting" (350). But K. is in dead sleep. Bürgel philosophizes, "This is indeed an excellent, time and again unimaginably excellent arrangement, even if in other respects dismal and cheerless" (351).

What can one say? Was he the loophole? The irony of the situation is the fairy tale's disclaimer. Bürgel is the author's deus ex machina come down to taunt the reader. Are not we being sported with as well as K.? "The essential is to go on squirming forever at the end of the line."[12]

What drives K.? What is the Castle? "[T]he unthinkable unspeakable" (*The Unnamable* 335) reward for bravery? The validation of his sacred "I"? Some truth that will free him to call off his quest without failing? Or, mischief à la Bürgel and the Castle? A travail designed for the "it" they would have him admit to being? "[A] punishment for having been born" (*The Unnamable* 310)? So we are asked to stand with K. and the Unnamable in their folly against bastards.

The Unnamable is the inverse of *The Castle*; the struggle to go forward to salvation has become the struggle to go backward to salvation. Success is not the issue; there is no getting there. There is in fact nowhere to get, no "quittance" into a place of reward. But the worlds in which these heroic follies are enacted are different to the extent that one is bright and theatrical and the other frantic. *The Trial* is not bright and funny. It is *The Castle*, especially, that Beckett has in mind when discussing his art in relation to Kafka's.

I've only read Kafka in German—serious reading—except for a few things in French and English—only "The Castle" in German.

I must say it was difficult to get to the end. The Kafka hero has a coherence of purpose. He's lost but he's not spiritually precarious, he's not falling to bits. My people seem to be falling to bits. Another difference [which is the same difference more sharply defined]. You notice how Kafka's form is classic, it goes on like a steamroller—almost serene. *It seems* to be threatened the whole time—but the consternation is in the form. In my work there is consternation behind the form, not in the form.[13]

"[C]onsternation . . . in the form," thinking of *The Castle*, is a never-ending circle around a starting point with no dismay on the part of the hero. "[C]onsternation behind the form" implies a hero struggling against hopelessness. Beckett's description fits K. of *The Castle*, not Joseph K. of *The Trial*, who is falling to pieces. K. is unflappable; the Unnamable is desperate with consternation but will not fall to pieces. The resemblance and affinity between *The Castle* and *The Unnamable* lies in the lessons Beckett learned from Kafka about what it takes to continue the senseless pantomime while maintaining the reader's sympathy for the hero as well as the spirit of comedy. *The Unnamable* is *The Castle* inside out. K. is like Adam in his infancy going through the paces for the first time. The Unnamable is cycles old. In both worlds, everything is stacked against them—everyone is their enemy. The one goes forward, bright and naïve as a billiard ball; the other struggles backward, indefatigably dodging.

The two novels tell the same intrinsic story about a hero questing for something unattainable and beset by enemies. The quest is the motive force of the hero's being. It is his being—his sacred "I." Everything about their situations ministers to the "I" slipping away. The process of thought itself can be invidious. Kafka's hero is not reflective, and Kafka keeps him that way, which is why K. seems almost serene. The Unnamable knows why thinking is dangerous: thought tends to be a palliative. The effort to understand one's situation, conceptualize, portray, take control, place oneself above oneself, minimizes the fear, dulls the pain, stereotypes one's struggle—it's treacherous. With enemies within and without, it is hard not to let go and lose one's meaning, and sink into the anonymity of human existence. The "I" can do nothing but somehow hold out against the forces arraigned against it. No love, no trusting alliances, no being knitted into community, no real succor, not even a doormat for dirty feet. Struggling on is a matter of conditioning. It's got to become a reflex—the mind in relentless high gear, racing, paranoid, vigilant, obsessive, the individual always fugitive. It's no life; the heroes have no defenses; they have no real hopes. All they can do is try to go on.

Truth need not be an issue to the reader, though the minds of both heroes may be similar to that of a schizophrenic. Paranoia is presented as a survival skill to a mind alert to the sacredness of self and the manifold threats to its existence. The hero lives—the precious fragile flame burns—only so long as he can keep struggling on. Be agog, poets, these are the epic poems of our time—how K. and the Unnamable persevere not to disappear, or, to "smother in a throng" (*The Unnamable* 292).

Their situation is like that of a rat treading water in a pail; they must struggle or drown. Going on means remaining as near as possible to a vestige of oneself. Thinking is dangerous (as noted) if used for the immediate reinforcements afforded by fictionalizing one's situation, including respite and momentary escape from the feeling of continuously being at bay. The return to oneself from such relaxation is perilous. Telling stories only weakens one, for a big motive underlying the need is self-pity—the reaching out for companionship, understanding, consolation. In every way storytelling is a corruption of one's will. No, nix to the powerful need to be soothed. That's why the heroes of the Unnamable's canonical fictions, Molloy and Malone, are deadbeat loners. That's why K. is a disreputable loner.

Thinking is the most formidable enemy of the hero. K. instinctively closes his mind and breasts forward. The Unnamable knows its pitfalls, which doesn't mean he can avoid them. Most invidious, perhaps, is protective thinking—planning ahead, engineering a strategy. Spotting a regulative intention behind one's moves—that is, catching sight of oneself mechanized—must destroy one's will to go on. Being, for the two heroes, is a saga of relentless dodging and continuous forays and the finding of sources of energy. They must be on their toes, dancing, so to say, on the edge. No hideaway corners, no fortifications. The strength to go on lies in their amazing resilience.

After the romantic poets and the modernists, Beckett, following Kafka, took the next giant step toward validating the sacredness of the self, operating in a world wherein existence had become inimical to the sacred.

K. is born into the world of the Castle as into an incomprehensible fairy tale. K.'s course of action becomes a process of discovery. It is that way with a dream; one never knows what could arise. He presumes to be the Land-Surveyor summoned by the Castle; in the village his reputation has preceded him. He meets with suspicion and hostility. There is no foreshadowing, there can be no anticipation, only the complications of the emerging circumstances and K.'s efforts to circumvent all obstacles. After a futile rush on the Castle, he finds two men waiting for him at the inn whom the innkeeper introduces as his assistants. He has no assistants and yet they exist; they claim to be his assistants and he accepts them. He saw them coming from the Castle; they do not deny it. They have no equipment with them; they make no explanation. They admit they know nothing about surveying. Having difficulty distinguishing one from the other, he says to them, "You're as like as two snakes" (24). Assistants they may be, but at the same time he feels them to be enemies. Getting to the Castle is the destination, but nothing else is predetermined. There is no path; yet randomness and the absurd seem to pave the way. He orders his assistants to get the sleigh ready in the morning to take him to the Castle. The impetus to get to the Castle is involuntary and overriding. All his actions are efforts to build bridges; the form wells up continuously as a series of barriers. The inverse is true for the Unnamable, who erects his own barriers so as not to be thrust outward from the black void that is his comparative refuge into the great futility, "among the incriminated scenes, tottering under the attributes peculiar to the lords of creation, dumb with howling to be put out of my misery" (*The Unnamable* 315–16). "The essential is never to arrive anywhere, never to be anywhere" (338). Just the opposite is true for K., who at once tries to penetrate the Castle unnoticed.

It is a given that deflection from K.'s purpose means being destroyed—precisely the situation of the Unnamable. He feels no gratitude to the one family of well-wishers in the village, for he believes they cannot help him. His reaction to useless kindness towards him is aversion. He has no principles. Lying, deception, flattery, and betrayal come automatically to serve his end.

Nevertheless he has our allegiance. For all the good it does him, we may be his only allies. Even Frieda, the wild, burning, carefree, delightful girl who spurns Klamm's summons (Klamm, the ultrahigh Castle official, the Master in the fairy tale), crying aloud that she is with the Land-Surveyor, and who carries K. into a whirlwind of sexual delirium, is diabolical in her pretense of innocence betrayed. She deserts K. on grounds of carnal treachery that she, not he, is guilty of, in point of fact. Other disclosures about her give us a pretext for sticking to K. even though he is desperately eager to sell her to Klamm. The issue for us is not K.'s character but his not losing his meaning. He must always keep his aim before him, ruthless against surplus emotions. The love of Frieda, Klamm's mistress, gives him a kind of whispering intimacy with (to put it plainly) the master of his fate. K.'s life-force is directed at closing the separation between him and Klamm who, through Frieda, means penetration into the Castle.

To be denied penetration, to be expelled into birth—to be annihilated: comparison between the two novels works to strengthen our allegiance to each of the heroes. To view one world from the other, *The Castle* from the vantage point of the trilogy, is like providing glasses with magical properties. The baffling and contradictory about K.'s world become plain. The importance of *The Castle* to the genesis of the trilogy becomes clear. Wearing Beckett's glasses, we recognize treachery that K. in his single-mindedness cannot see and sense conspiracy to which he is oblivious.

K. cannot believe that his violent treatment and banishment of the assistants are responsible for Frieda's haggardness. He thinks she longs for Klamm; she is precious to him on that account, "you miss Klamm and that gives you desperate ideas" (180). These are caressive words; her willingness to accommodate a deal engenders them. Frieda tells him that the assistants have been hungering after her like animals. K. finds himself defending them. She wrings her hands, "It's their deceit" (181). K. is insistent. He *will* believe that Frieda misses Klamm. Frieda states unambiguously that she cannot resist the assistants sexually, and then, surprise, she turns the tables on him. She does not wish to be tortured by her attraction to them, but if K. shuts them out he will lose forever the hope of gaining admittance to Klamm. "I want to save you by any means at all from such consequences" (184), rather neatly playing his hand to gain hers, "sacrificing" herself to the assistants to help K. to Klamm just as K. is willing to give her to Klamm to help him to the Castle. They're both being false to each other, but Frieda's shrewd move threatens K. with the wreckage of his plans. This dangerous turn of events K. rejects. He will not hear it. What saddens him, he says, is the extent to which she is still Klamm's sweetheart. We root for the folly of his single-mindedness. The comic spirit of the novel depends on our loyalty. Both comic spirit and loyalty depend on K.'s remaining undeflectable. There can be no end to his belief in his mission, other than "to stand like a beggar before the threshold, to one side of the entrance, to rot and collapse."[14] K. caresses Frieda, seeking the nearness to Klamm. Her rejection of him comes inevitably. It is definitive and perhaps intended for the crushing blow. In contrast to K., the Unnamable has learned to trust his paranoia, to beware of all alliances. "They want me roots and all" (352).

All K.'s enemies would deflate and crush him by making him feel small and by picturing his unequal struggle, but of all the sadists, K.'s educators, the worst is Olga. The others, the junta—the teacher, Mayor, Bridge Inn landlady, Momus, Erlanger, and Klamm himself—seem transparent by comparison to Olga. Frieda, too, like Olga, may be diabolical in innocence, indeed no friend to K., perhaps his worst enemy, but there is no "perhaps" about Olga. She is Castle bait to tempt K. to depend on her. She has experience of the Castle. Her brother, Barnabas, is a Castle messenger. All her revelations are speaking pictures of the hopelessness of K.'s quest, but framed as helpful, in alliance with K.'s single-minded aim. When he resists the infusion of futility, growing irritable rather than demoralized, his vehemence surprises her. Nothing Olga can tell him about Castle procedure can make him feel hopeless. So she maneuvers, and tries again to make herself his indispensable crutch—to become, in a manner of speaking, his double. Basil, in the analogous situation, speaks for and professes to be the Unnamable. K. is intended to hear a preview of his own fate in Olga's story of the great wrong done her family by the Castle.

Three years before they were prosperous, her parents were youthful. One morning a messenger delivered a letter from Castle officialdom summoning Olga's younger sister to come at once to the Herrenhof. Sortini had sent a brutally lewd letter threatening consequences if she disobeyed. Amalia tore Sortini's letter in pieces and threw it in the messenger's face. K. declares, bravo, Amalia, as if he did not know the consequences of Amalia's indignation—the doddering father, the family reputation, Amalia's ill health. Feeling that she has him hooked, Olga makes an aggressive move at overthrowing his base of support and plan. She tells him there is no difference between Klamm and Sortini, Frieda and Amalia, except that Frieda was obliging. Klamm, she says, has an even greater reputation for brutality.

However, K. rears up, antagonized by the comparison, and accuses Olga of trying to shake his confidence in Frieda. "[E]very attack on Frieda is an attack on myself" (258), meaning, as well, or primarily, you're obviously mistaken about Klamm. Don't touch there, he warns. K.'s vexation is aggressive; his existence is being attacked.

Instantly Olga turns his aggression aside by apologizing and by admitting her family is itself to blame for its circumstances. Having pacified him, she tries again to make herself indispensable by letting him know that she's prepared to do absolutely anything for him. She tells him that she's been sleeping with the servants of the Herrenhof stable in an effort to find Sortini's messenger and beg him to forgive the offense. Is it clear? She wants to break K.; all his enemies want the same. Olga wants him abjectly clinging to her. Moreover, his despair would be sweet revenge on Frieda, who will fuel her own betrayal of K. on the treachery of his needing Olga.

The Unnamable recognizes peril to his independence in the stories he restrains himself from telling. His needs, his predicament, his urgency, expressed in the form of a story, tend to solidify him into a stereotype. Telling stories encourages his abdication of himself, of his consciousness and suffering. His characters would beckon him to destruction, "chang[ing] me a little more each time into what [they] wanted me to be" (*The Unnamable* 298). They become inseparable from the junta of sadists and educators, training him—tutoring him into condition for human life, which in Beckett is synonymous with the concentration camp world, a death-in-life. Each of K.'s dramatic interactions is a story, the story of K. and Frieda, the story of K. and Olga. Every encounter in his struggle to persevere to the Castle is story-time—Kafka's story, Kafka himself telling his own story, K. being his stand-in; moreover a weakened Kafka, spiritually ill and dying, representing something like his life's journey—that is, going on while somehow keeping despair at bay, and possibly achieving apotheosis through writing. The trick of survival, of maintaining independence, of going on—the Unnamable has learned it—is to play out this need to represent oneself, this unstoppable urge to create fictions about oneself, in parody. If you must fictionalize your situation, show yourself to be unflappable. Play your story as cabaret if not screaming farce.

Are not K. and the surrounding cast performing cabaret, a theatrical "this is your life, Kafka," featuring a sexually experienced Kafka impervious to self-doubt and self-torment, the parody of a Kafka single-minded in his objectives, free of ambivalence; a cabaret musical on Kafka's lifelong efforts to get somewhere with his writing and the farce of there being somewhere to get to; a spoof on a Kafka who is not tortured by the world, but is a conniver jousting in a conniving world, with the author backing his rogue? Is not Klamm the master of the performance pulling all the strings? Olga may be right in comparing Klamm to Sortini, for it may dawn upon the reader that Frieda, Klamm's mistress, is also Klamm's daughter by the Bridge Inn landlady. K.'s independence and his presumption that he has rights goad the landlady into trying to bring him down, though the sharper motive for her malice is Castle intrigue—curiosity to see what will bring him down and when. All K.'s connections, everyone he meets, are servants of the Castle. Yet his very being, his K.-ness, is his genius of effrontery, just as the two Mahoods are the Unnamable's expressions of effrontery, testifying to his (like K.'s) unconquerable spirit. They are inassimilable. Beckett's stance in the trilogy (quintessentially in *Molloy*) is Kafkaesque, as in *The Castle*.

The Castle is written in a jauntier, cleaner spirit than *The Trial*. Joseph K.'s case in *The Trial* is before his conscience, which is a lost one the moment it becomes one. Malone is the Promethean exception, holding out against the Furies. Whatever K. of *The Castle* is seeking, his acquiescence to a sense of hopelessness is not a foregone conclusion. Joseph K. submits to "torture ... arising from his case and concomitant with it"[15]—arising, that is, from the secretly confessed, guilty side of his ambivalence. The torture is self-inflicted. The machine's operation is given in an elaborate set piece.

Alone in his office on a winter day, he sits motionless with bowed head reexamining the progress of his case. The first pleas in his case were ready for presentation. They could be crucial; then again they might not be read, though that was a rumor, though not wholly without justification. The charge sheets were inaccessible to the accused and his counsel; this meant that an effective first plea was highly improbable. Effective pleas could not be written until much later on. Actually, the defense was not countenanced by the law, only tolerated, and with contempt at that. The law-court office for the attorneys was in a cranny of the attic with a hole in the floor that the lawyers were prohibited from repairing. The Court wanted to eliminate defending counsel as much as possible, and to put the onus of the offense on the accused themselves. However, it would be a big mistake to suppose that accused persons do not need lawyers. They were especially necessary before this Court in which records and proceedings were kept secret and counsel prohibited from interrogations. The most important thing in the process of a trial before this Court was counsel's connections. In that lay the chief value of the defense, although these important intimates were mere functionaries who could not be counted on to follow through on what they said in private. Nor had they any understanding of human relations, which in cases like Joseph K.'s was indispensable. They were notoriously irritable and capricious because of the secret proceedings of the Court, which made it impossible for them to follow the progress of their cases. Just about everything important to the case was outside their jurisdiction. But, thanks to the lawyer, the accused knew more about his case than these officials. These were the conditions, and the only sensible thing

was to adapt oneself to them. For despite appearances, everything interlocked and remained unchanged, except for more
severe and rigorous punishments on would-be reformers. Joseph
K. should know that he had already greatly damaged his case;
although, it may be, only cases predestined to succeed from the
start came to a good end, while the rest were doomed to fail. At
any rate, nothing was yet lost.

The Joseph K. of *The Trial* is in danger of being overtaken by
"the screaming silence of no's knife in yes's wound" (*Texts for
Nothing* 139). His every denial of guilt deepens his mortal acquiescence to it. He might try to ward off judgment, to keep the
steam up for awhile, but his options are not to his taste—a
choice of tortures. "[O]stensible acquittal" (*The Trial* 191)—
Malone's life is a perfect example—means to refuse guilt and attempt to live freely. It means surviving continuous arrests. "The
second acquittal is followed by the third arrest, the third acquittal by the fourth arrest, and so on" (200). "[I]ndefinite postponement" (191) consists in preventing the case from making progress. This means continuously remaining in touch with the
Court. The advantage of this second option lies in less "strain
and agitation" (201). At the same time there is no pretense of
being free. The accused acknowledges the status of his case
before the Court and his case never leaves his mind. He can go
on into exhaustion pawning away his life to keep hope alive.

But *The Castle* is the production of a different Kafka. K. cannot be made to feel hopeless like Joseph K. Joseph K. is falling to
pieces and one feels his consternation. This crucial difference between the two K.s helped Beckett to his stance in each part of
the trilogy.

The ideas that Beckett harvested from *The Castle* include the
following: The struggle is to survive; survival is a given. Falling
to pieces is a symptom of capitulation. And if one has come to
the point of falling to pieces, one must nevertheless struggle to
be true to the ruins one has made of one's life. Let it be a martyrdom not to lose self-possession. Since the hero cannot "live,
with their kind of life, for a single second" (*The Unnamable* 334),
then have no conscience, conscience is guilt. Have no past, no
memories "misted and smeared with the filth of years" (*Malone
Dies* 198): suppress them relentlessly. Best to be pastless, un-

hampered, complete. Refuse to be, in the Christian ethos, one of the sheep, no matter how black. Uphold irreverence and blasphemy. Belonging means perishing. Life being unspeakable, make no compromises with it. Be disreputable, solitary, smelly. Make mockery of the disposition to nest. Above all, cheekiness—play, wit, fertility of invention, jokes that cascade into a series of punch lines, clownishness, comic routines: song and dance to one's own tunes rather than wriggling to the beat of others'.

Molloy's narrative has the logic of a musical score. It is Kafka-esque, as in *The Castle*, in which laughter and song are always "audible"—the dialogues similarly stagy, as in a theatrical farce, having about them the exaggerated stylization of performance, and invariably on the verge of parodic inflation, as in comic routines. Perhaps the cleanest fun for the reader is the carnival scene the evening of the second day in the crowded, unruly inn, loud with suppressed laughter, when K. receives official notice that he's been engaged by the Castle; and the scenes immediately following, the lovemaking in the taproom, and the interview with the Mayor, before the game afoot is known. By dusk of the fourth day, the buffeting becomes relentless.

K. makes for the Herrenhof, to the bar, to the very door behind which Klamm had been when K. met Frieda. The door is locked and he looks for the peephole. He has banked on his engagement to Frieda to get him access to Klamm. He contemplates the barmaid, Pepi, "greedily" (131), considering what he might use her for. Moments later he is standing in the inn's courtyard looking at a closed sleigh to which a pair of horses are hitched. Eating a sandwich prepared for him by Frieda, thinking gratefully of her solicitous provision for him, he waits to waylay Klamm. He enters Klamm's closed sleigh, caresses the luxurious pillowed interior, and spills a flask of brandy on the carpet. He refuses to leave the field. Shortly the horses are unhitched and the courtyard deserted. When finally he withdraws in defeat, which in some way feels like a triumph, he finds the Bridge Inn landlady crouched before a keyhole hoping to catch a glimpse of the departing Klamm. K. is then taunted by her up yeses and down nos of his hopes regarding Klamm. Henceforth it is all torture, or would be if it were possible to knock the wind out of K.'s sails.

Barnabas arrives with a letter from Klamm claiming to be highly pleased with K.'s work as Land-Surveyor. This sadistic tease causes momentary consternation. "I can't even excite the gentleman's displeasure" (156). Agitated but undaunted, K. dispatches Barnabas to beseech Klamm for a private meeting. Beckett's Unnamable also struggles to hold on to the fairy tale of the good master, despite evidence of his ill will.

The next day K. is disturbed by Frieda's anxious solicitude for the assistants. This blows up. He refuses her plea that they leave the village, refuses to hear of her attraction to the assistants, refuses her warning not to neglect her in his weary business with Klamm.

He hurries off to Barnabas's house hoping to intercept a letter from Klamm, and remains there spellbound by Olga. There he receives a psychological battering lasting for hours, interrupted only at three in the morning by a loud knocking on the door. As if playing in a command performance engineered somehow by the Castle, he is challenged by the assistant Jeremiah for treachery to Frieda. K. would kick him aside, were it not for the fact that Jeremiah had come as Frieda's lover with news of her desertion.

K. is turned about by the entrance of Barnabas with a message for him from one of Klamm's chief secretaries, Erlanger: "Report to Herrenhof instanter." There is no letup. The unfoldings run on at a supercharged pace. Yet K.'s crisis at the Herrenhof remains funny, partly because the consternation is in the scene, the situation, the serenity of the prose, and because he continues on, undiminished.

K. spots and woos Frieda and loses her. There is no doubt that she has left him for good. He is without a single ally. It is possible he never had one. He accidentally enters Bürgel's room in blank exhaustion. Perhaps, too, this tease of a loophole is engineered by the Castle.

The sadists are in full swing ready to bring out the champagne. Then Erlanger, to Castle laughter, shafts K., commanding him to facilitate Frieda's return to the taproom immediately. Erlanger knows Frieda has been reinstalled; he knows everything. So he taunts K.—Klamm may be used to her attendance and disturbed by her absence. Favors are hinted at for K.'s compliance "in this trivial affair" (354).

Kafka, in one of his deletions, looked at K. from the angle of Castle officialdom: "He's always in raptures over such a summons, in this respect disappointments have no effect on him—if only one could learn that from him! Each new summons reinforces, not his old disappointments, but only his old hope" (424). No, he can't be driven away, any more than cockroaches can be driven away.

A new scene soon unfolds, a commotion in the corridor, which thoroughly absorbs K. It is the distribution of files, K.'s case possibly among them, the great piles of bound documents being carted from door to door by a servant and assistant. Bundles are left, hotly negotiated for, refused, flung at the opposite wall; secretaries stubbornly and noisily vie with one another for the most files. This preposterous disorder elicits admiration from K. for the cunning and skill of the servant in dealing "with these stubborn little rooms" (360). The servant, too, never gives up.

The scene ends with his eviction from the passage by landlord and landlady together; his impropriety was intolerable. There would be consequences.

After twelve hours of deep sleep nestled on a beer keg, K. is caressed by the plump, round-shouldered barmaid Pepi. She tells K. that she dreamed of his leaving Frieda for her. What was he after? She would readily sacrifice herself for him. He could only have been attracted to Frieda because of Klamm. Klamm was the reason for Frieda's superior airs. Pepi knew her to be artful and a liar and plain to the point of being ugly—"that skinny, sallow thing" (388). What possible appeal could she have had for Klamm? And supposing it so, why would she throw herself away on a nonentity like K.? Little Pepi, full of spite, offers dimly shrewd disclosures. Did Klamm take on Frieda for the novelty of possessing both his concubine and his daughter? Did he summon her from the Bridge Inn and install her in the taproom for his convenience? Did he request her to seduce K., live bait for Castle fun? Was she all the while in dirty intrigue with the assistants? Is it slyly, caressively that Pepi confides that as barmaid she too has her fantasy? She pined for Klamm. She invites K. to live with her and two other chambermaids in a cozy room off the secretaries' passage, until spring at least. He accepts the proposition.

In a final scene bright with easy comedy, the landlady of the Herrenhof flirts with K. who had given her a backhanded compliment on her wardrobe (outmoded, outlandish clothes). "I am only aiming at dressing beautifully, and you are either a fool or a child or a very wicked, dangerous person," and she shouts after him, "I am getting a new dress tomorrow, perhaps I shall send for you" (412). K. has the advantage—at least momentarily.

With this peal of laughter the novel ends—appropriately, I think. Max Brod, Kafka's close friend and biographer, claims (in the first American edition) that Kafka told him K. was to die in the village worn out by his struggle and that after his death word was to come from the Castle permitting him to live and to work there. But that's to give the Castle the final word, the last laugh—"He's mewled, he'll rattle," etc., "they all let themselves be saved, they all let themselves be born" (*The Unnamable* 383)—in what for K., as for the Unnamable, are fights to maintain a sense of self and not be degraded.

The Unnamable, then, is K. beyond the grave, present as thought coursing at varying speeds through an intricate grid of interconnecting ideas—rushing along byways of associations, counting on what comes along to keep going, dodging despair and the pressure to expel him into life. The pressure is relentless; yet no cage can catch this wily bird flashing by like tracer sparks. "I am he who will never be caught, never delivered" (*The Unnamable* 339).

At this point we might remind our readers of the dangers threatening the Unnamable's morale. For example, he must not tell stories. Stories are perilous because they encourage his conscription to life. And they sour him; the fall back into himself, his refuge, is hard. But he feels secure when his voice is raised in parody. So he creates the adventures of the two Mahoods, which are the whoops of a soul delighting in freedom. And he conceives Worm, unawakened matter, and describes its nativity, whose *Soul cometh from afar*. "[T]he rot spreads downwards, soon he'll have legs" (355). Lured from a deep pit, hooked on a long pole, "There he is now with breath in his nostrils, it only remains for him to suffocate" (355).

But how long can this go on; how long can the hero hold out?—no doubt the thought prompting Brod's question to Kafka, how was *The Castle* to end? If we look at the passage of crisis in *The Unnamable*, we see what brings it on—see, that is, in that tremendous evocation of despair, that the disarming blow is a clear perception of futility. The grid of his random, seemingly chaotic movements, has penetrated his consciousness; he perceives the play, visualizes it in all its intricacies as being repetitive. Going on has become torture, pure and simple:

> there is nothing to be done, nothing special to be done, nothing doable to be done. . . . no point in telling yourself stories, to pass the time, stories don't pass the time, nothing passes the time . . . trying to cease and never ceasing, seeking the cause, the cause of talking and never ceasing, finding the cause, losing it again, finding it again, not finding it again, seeking no longer, seeking again, finding again, losing again, finding nothing, finding at last, losing again, talking without ceasing, thirstier than ever, seeking as usual, losing as usual, blathering away, wondering what it's all about, seeking what it can be you are seeking, exclaiming, Ah yes, sighing. No no, crying, Enough, ejaculating, Not yet, talking incessantly, any old thing, seeking once more, any old thing, thirsting away, you don't know what for, ah yes, something to do, no no, nothing to be done . . . talking unceasingly, seeking incessantly, in yourself, outside yourself, cursing man, cursing God, stopping cursing, past bearing it, going on bearing it, seeking indefatigably, . . . what are you seeking, who is seeking, seeking who you are, supreme aberration, where you are, what you're doing, what you've done to them, what they've done to you, prattling along, where are the others, who is talking, not I, where am I, where is the place where I've always been, where are the others, it's they are talking, talking to me, talking of me, I hear them, I'm mute, what do they want, what have I done to them, what have I done to God, what have they done to God, what has God done to us . . . rattling on, dying of thirst, seeking determinedly, what they want, they want me to be, this, that, to howl, stir, crawl out of here, be born, die, listen, I'm listening . . . the words are everywhere, inside me, outside me . . . impossible to stop them, impossible to stop, I'm in words, made of words . . . nothing ever but me, a particle of me, retrieved, lost, gone astray, I'm all these words . . . yes, something else, that I'm something quite different, a quite different thing, a wordless thing in an empty place, a hard shut dry cold black place, where nothing stirs, nothing speaks, and that I listen, and that I seek, like a caged beast born of caged beasts

born of caged beasts born of caged beasts born in a cage and dead
in a cage, born and then dead, born in a cage and then dead in a
cage, in a word like a beast . . . (385–87)

What is the point of struggling on? The answer is the same as
it always has been—to be himself, not to suffer degradation. If
he relinquishes the futile hope that words will enable him to
probe the mystery of his core self—if he caves in to the necessity
of being born—he becomes that beast caught in the cycle of gen-
eration, a prisoner of matter. Once born the self would no longer
be worth knowing. Take me, he says, take me, web of folly and
pain, as he prays for the magical words that will release him
through the doorway held open by the master. And so he goes on
relentlessly, against futility, helped out by a fairy tale.

5

The Kafka we imagine is made up of refractions of a torturing
ambivalence, a wounded being like Joseph K. of *The Trial*, whose
torment is self-inflicted. Within this Kafka, the version informed
by his diaries, letters, aphorisms, indeed, by everything he
wrote, one can imagine the dim presence of another Kafka who
has broken away from himself into Beckett's fiction—coming
into being in the *Nouvelles*, established as a being in Molloy; established perhaps even in Malone, a new version of Job holding
out against being reduced to Kafka. In the Unnamable, Kafka is
himself again, but not quite—tortured but not guilty; hopeless,
but driven; inexhaustible. *The Unnamable* can be seen as a tribute to the Kafka capable of creating *The Castle* despite incurable
illness and despair.

As suggested in chapter 5, the prose-poem sequence *Texts for
Nothing* (1951) might be dedicated to Kafka. The torment of ambivalence it evokes was Kafka's as well as Beckett's when in
1946 he turned to Kafka's example to break out of his own spiritual deadlock and write the trilogy. To both, the plight of the
artist was hopeless. Inspiration depends upon the separation
from life and the contradictory longing to be in the world he despises. If he joins the world, he would cease to exist as a writer.
Also in despising the world, he ceases to exist as a writer. The

artist is condemned to observe and oscillate, desiring the unbearable in an inferno of shifting moods that is his imaginative life. Beckett's *Texts for Nothing* evokes this oscillation. It tells of the inevitable dying out of the imagination while attesting to an unstoppable creative drive.

In 1911, Kafka wrote of his

> fear of betraying . . . self-perception. This fear is justified, for one should permit a self-perception to be established definitively in writing only when it can be done with the greatest completeness, with all the incidental consequences, as well as with entire truthfulness. For if this does not happen—and in any event I am not capable of it—then what is written down will, in accordance with its own purpose and with the superior power of the established, replace what has been felt only vaguely in such a way that the real feeling will disappear while the worthlessness of what has been noted down will be recognized too late. (*Diaries 1910–1913* 41)

This may be the clearest statement of the pensum, the burden, with its command to go on, that lies behind Beckett's, like Kafka's, unstoppable creative drive: kept going by the pipe dream of the master waiting to reward you for speaking the truth, for finding the way through the labyrinth of self to the intrinsic "I." In the writer versus world ambivalence—seemingly exaggerated into parody in Kafka's volume of letters to Felice—the anguishing issue behind the list of pro's and con's to marriage is that bedrock truth about himself. Confess the truth, scum. Guilt, bankruptcy are the truth. *The Trial* is nothing but a procrastination of judgment, a farcical process of yesing noes to guilt and to a submission that is shameful.

For Kafka, opting for either side of his ambivalence was folly, but the daring surrender to his writing had its redeeming aspect. To Max Brod and especially Ronald Hayman, among his biographers, *The Castle* represents Kafka's quest for salvation through writing. And this also may be Thomas Mann's intimation when speaking of K.'s relentless, unstoppable, destructive, absurd questing for an imaginary beatitude.[16]

"Ostensible acquittal" (applied to Kafka's life) is the forestalling of judgment by writing. Judgment is irrevocable, but ostensible acquittal is less ignominious than "Indefinite postponement," which is hiding behind skirts.

During one of his engagements to Felice, Kafka told Brod, "I ought to be whipped out into the desert."[17] And Kafka felt no less ignominious for living with his parents instead of alone with his writing. Letters like the following one to Felice, interesting as literature, stand out in that court of assize where the final verdict has already come down, as examples of squirming faithless cowardice: "My life is made up of two parts, the one feeds on your life with bulging cheeks and could be in itself happy and a great man; but the other part is like a cobweb come adrift; being free of tension, free of headaches is its supreme though not too frequent joy."[18]

For most of his life, Kafka lived with his parents and five other adults in a crowded apartment. At the end of his life in Berlin, he escaped, more or less, "a stranger among strangers, with no past or future to entrap him."[19] Bravo Kafka: free of the hooks of the Court, Joseph K. becomes like K. of *The Castle*, and thus bears the germ of resemblance to Molloy.

Molloy is unmistakable in the self-portrait Kafka drew for Felice and also copied in his diary in 1916:

> Having as a rule depended on others, I have an infinite longing for independence, self-reliance, freedom in all directions; I would rather wear blinkers and go my own way to the bitter end, than have my vision distorted by being in the midst of frenzied family life. . . . Any relationship not created by myself, even though it be opposed to parts of my own nature, is worthless; it hinders my movements, I hate it, or come near to hating it. . . . Yet, I am my parents' progeny, am bound to them . . . by blood. . . . Sometimes this too becomes the object of my hatred; at home the sight of the double bed, of sheets that have been slept in, of nightshirts carefully laid out, can bring me to the point of retching, can turn my stomach inside out; it is as though my birth had not been final, as though from this fusty life I keep being born again and again in this fusty room; as though I had to return there for confirmation, being—if not quite, at least in part—indissolubly connected with these distasteful things; something still clings to the feet as they try to break free, held fast as they are in the primeval slime.[20]

This is a good description of why Molloy cannot break free of his mother. The conscience of Malone is portrayed in Molloy, who cannot escape the crime of his birth, or his mother. Kafka wanted to hate the father he loved. Molloy wants to hate the mother he loves and cannot forgive or forget. Moran represses the mother he cannot hate and displaces hatred onto the world. Maybe a crux of *Molloy* lies in the contrast between bad (Molloy's narrative) and worse (Moran's narrative) life sentences.

The worst sentence is reserved for the Kafka who lived with his parents. Ernst Pawel, Kafka's biographer, says of "The Metamorphosis," "it is a poisoned fairy tale about the magic of hate and the power of hypocrisy."[21] Can the same be said of Beckett's *Nouvelles*—transformations into flotsam? There is no hypocrisy in those deadbeat heroes and what force of judgment there is in the *Nouvelles* concerns the world. *First Love, The Expelled, The End*, and *The Calmative* describe the tenure of a man's life with no past or future to entrap him. "[I]t is such a predetermined state of being in and for itself, stripped of all trimmings that could help him by distorting life—distorting it in the direction of beauty or of misery, no matter."[22] This is Milena Jesenská's view of Kafka, though she might be talking about Beckett's deadbeats. She was Kafka's Czech translator. In 1922, after an intense but unconsummated affair, he gave her all his diaries. Milena's words are a kind of confirmation that one could think of Kafka in the way I am suggesting that Beckett did, in developing from the *Nouvelles* to the trilogy.

> I rather think that all of us, each and every one of us, is sick and that he is the only well person, the only one who sees rightly and feels rightly, the only pure person. I know that he does not resist *life*, but only *this kind of life*: that is what he resists. . . . And yet there is not another person in the whole world who has his tremendous strength.[23]

Milena's description of Kafka could describe Molloy and Malone.

To Kafka, both the inability to live in the world and the ability to accommodate the world are indictments. To Beckett, birth makes failure inevitable. The trilogy presents an aesthetics for survival that is not found in Kafka until *The Castle*. Joseph K. is impaled from the time of his arrest, crippled, rendered anomalous, conscious. Does he want the old condition of life again? Those stricken with consciousness are ambivalent. Put in the position of holding tight to a suffocating space that is prima facie evidence of guilt, they have two options, one of which is less ignominious. Reading Kafka through Beckett is to introduce a third option, the least ignominious, if not positively noble under the terms of existence: Molloy and Malone. They exchange the world for an aesthetics of vagrancy and martyrdom.

When a fellow patient at a sanitarium dying of tuberculosis of the larynx asked Kafka to look at the abscesses in his throat, which he exhibited by manipulating mirrors, Kafka nearly fainted. "[N]o man dares to torture the way [life does]," he wrote Brod.

> and—the unique element—the victim himself is compelled, by his own will, out of his own wretched inner self, to protract the torture. . . . And his relatives and the doctors and visitors have literally built some scaffoldings over this not burning but slowly smouldering pyre, so that without danger of contagion they can visit, cool, and comfort the tormented man, cheer him up to endure further misery. (*Letters to Friends* 253–54)

"[F]ilthy, filthy," was his verdict some weeks later to Brod, "all of it filthy" (*Letters to Friends* 287). To Beckett, Kafka would have been looking life straight in the eye. Malone looks it straight in the eye and continues to triumph over the temptation to moral flagellation.

Yet Kafka sought rest cures at sanatoriums, not for his tuberculosis, but for respite from his moral suffering. In Matliary (winter 1920–21), he sought to prolong his stay indefinitely. The world seemed remote; yet he would not forsake it. He must keep his job at the institute; his state of peaceful numbness depended upon the scaffolding of everyday life. He plotted a strategy: 1) He must ask for leave. 1a) He must write the director, Odstrčil asking his opinion on extending his leave. 1a1) He must write the letter in Czech, which meant submitting it to his brother-in-law for proofing. 1a2) He must deliberately make mistakes in his final draft because the director looked for mistakes in everything and he must find the necessary quota. 1a3) Depending on the director's answer, he would submit a petition. 2) But his leave had expired, he had waited too long. 2a) He writes his sister Ottla, mentioning that he would like to stay in Matliary but could not because he felt uneasy asking for yet another leave of absence. 2a1) But perhaps, hinting to his sister, Odstrčil on his own would write Kafka to take another year of leave. 2a2) He signs off his letter to Ottla forlorn, telling her that he would be back in Prague in a week since no such letter from Odstrčil was likely to arrive. 2b) At the last moment he writes Brod to run the errand he had intimated to Ottla, specifically to go to the institute for him and ask for two months leave with either full, three-quarter, or half pay. 2b1) He supplies instructions to Brod on how to approach the director. 2b2) He directs Max to check with his family first to make sure that Ottla had not already preceded him.[24]

The alternative to this degraded living on—on the Court's terms, anaesthetized to allow the torture to continue—was to live through his writing. But he had failed. "I have remained clay, I have not blown the spark into fire, but only used it to light up my corpse" (*Letters to Friends* 334). For two years, before beginning *The Castle* in early 1922, he was continuously on the verge of a mental breakdown. He had rejected the world. He had systematically destroyed himself to ensure an undistracted solitude. The result had been despair, illness, exhaustion, and worse, madness—the belief that there was no way out; the feeling that everything outside the elsewhere of his solitude—for example friends, work, family—was imaginary; that he was "beating [his] head against the wall of a windowless and doorless cell."[25]

Three axioms can be drawn from his last writings about being a writer (in "The Burrow," "A Hunger Artist," and "Josephine the Singer, or the Mouse Folk"): the writer writes in order to feel safe, though the activity is isolating, obsessional, and spiritually destructive. The writer writes in order to find satisfaction in disintegration. The writing may provide others with occasional entertainment beyond which it has no value. There is no way out—the writer is condemned to an elsewhere, cut off from and repelled by life, playing taps for his dying imagination—a situation also lamented by the writer narrator of *Texts for Nothing*.

Yet the writer's compulsion overrides even despair:

[Y]ou must go on, I can't go on, you must go on, I'll go on, you must say words, as long as there are any, until they find me, until they say me, strange pain, strange sin, you must go on, perhaps it's done already, perhaps they have said me already, perhaps they have carried me to the threshold of my story, before the door that opens on my story, that would surprise me, if it opens, it will be I. (*The Unnamable* 414)

K. emerges bringing the universe of the Castle with him, a celebration of the imagination to the um-pah-pah of a cabaret band. K. accepts the fluidity and uncertainty of his phenomenal world—no borders, no logic, no frame, no succor; a pantomime of hammering; a K. who pursues his quest without recalling its cause, unperturbed by his inability to do anything but circle about his starting point. He does not know the words to describe his non-journey. Question: Does the narrator intrude on the unfolding drama? Answer: Very rarely, only perhaps to further disabuse us of the notion of a stable point of view. Understanding is rejected, self-knowledge disappears. The hero is solipsistic; there is little in the way of memory and no emotion attached to it; a hero coming into being via his self-perceptions, who cannot impose any order on what he sees. Kafka the narrator can assert no real control or certitude about the story without risking the reader's allegiance to the hero and to the comic spirit of his hopeless quest. An objective point of view from either the narrator or K. would be fatal. The key word in this universe is "perhaps." Beckett incorporated these characteristics of Kafka's art into his own work. Beckett also might be thought a Talmudist, for he had in common with Kafka an ability to take ideas literally and pursue them relentlessly. And Beckett too was a master of that cannonade effect of exaggeration rumbling to absurdity over a series of clauses reminiscent of Kafka's well-known expression of his worthlessness: "a useless stake covered with snow and frost, fixed loosely and slantwise into the ground in a deeply plowed field on the edge of a great plain on a dark winter's night" (*Diaries 1914–1923* 100). The voice is unmistakable: "I whose soul writhed from morning to night, in the mere quest of itself";[26] "I'm too frightened this evening to listen to myself rot";[27] "I'm no longer with these assassins, in this bed of terror";[28] "I'm dead and getting born, without having ended, helpless to begin, that's my life";[29] "I'll have gone on giving up, having had nothing, not being there";[30] "And it's still the same old road I'm trudging, up yes and down no, towards one yet to be named, so that [they] may leave me in peace, be in peace, be no more, have never been."[31] This sounds like Kafka but is Beckett.

Notes

INTRODUCTION

1. Samuel Beckett, *Enough*, in *Samuel Beckett: The Complete Short Prose, 1929–1989*, ed. S. E. Gontarski (New York: Grove, 1995), 186–89, 191–92.

2. Ruby Cohn, *A Beckett Canon* (Ann Arbor: University of Michigan Press, 2001), 296.

3. Ibid., 307.

4. Ibid., 297.

5. James Knowlson and John Pilling, *Frescoes of the Skull: The Later Prose and Drama of Samuel Beckett* (New York: Grove, 1980), 153, 152.

6. Ibid., 155.

7. Enoch Brater thinks *Enough* is an artful interweave of multiple stories "competing for affirmation." Every reader will hear it differently, attenuating and textualizing—inventing. Any interpretation is another fiction, he says. Enoch Brater, *The Drama in the Text: Beckett's Late Fiction* (New York: Oxford University Press, 1994), 62.

Enough then is a riddle to which there is no right answer. In Brater's dramatic readings of the late prose, there are no stories to discern. "Playing with time, meter, rhyme, metaphor and, above all, diction, *Imagination Dead Imagine* lets us hear for the first of many times the importance that the sound of words acquires in its tension with unspoken experience" (89). For Brater, the late prose is abstract art.

8. I refer, of course, to William Blake's poem *The Book of Thel* (1789).

9. Martin Amis, *Experience* (New York: Hyperion, 2000), 82.

10. Samuel Beckett, *The Unnamable*, in *Three Novels: Molloy, Malone Dies, The Unnamable* (1955; reprint, New York: Grove, 1958), 292.

11. Samuel Beckett, *How It Is* (New York: Grove, 1964), 36.

12. Dante Alighieri, *Inferno*, in *The Divine Comedy*, ed. and trans. Robert M. Durling (New York: Oxford University Press, 1997), Canto 25 ll.1–3, 381.

13. Samuel Beckett, *The Lost Ones*, in *The Complete Short Prose*, 204.

CHAPTER 1: THE *NOUVELLES*

1. Ruby Cohn, *A Beckett Canon* (Ann Arbor: University of Michigan Press, 2001), 150.
2. Ibid., 131.
3. Ibid., 151.
4. Ibid., 133.
5. J. E. Dearlove, *Accommodating the chaos: Samuel Beckett's nonrelational art* (Durham, N.C.: Duke University Press, 1982), 56.
6. Ibid., 56.
7. Ibid., 60.
8. Ibid., 61.
9. Samuel Beckett, *First Love*, in *Samuel Beckett: The Complete Short Prose, 1929–1989*, ed. S. E. Gontarski (New York: Grove, 1995), 33.
10. Franz Kafka, "The Metamorphosis," *Franz Kafka: The Complete Stories*, ed. Nahum N. Glatzer (1946; reprint, New York: Schocken, 1983), 138.
11. Samuel Beckett, *The Expelled*, in *The Complete Short Prose,* 49.
12. Samuel Beckett, *The End*, in *The Complete Short Prose,* 81.
13. Samuel Beckett, *Stories* and *Texts for Nothing* (New York: Grove Weidenfeld, 1967), 108.
14. Samuel Beckett, *The Calmative*, in *The Complete Short Prose,* 61.
15. W. S. Merwin, letter to Roderick Townley, in *Night Errands: How Poets Use Dreams*, ed. Roderick Townley (Pittsburgh: University of Pittsburgh Press, 1998), 12.
16. I am indebted to Raymond Federman, who wrestles with the implications of Beckett's artistic stance in the *Nouvelles*, in *Journey to Chaos: Samuel Beckett's Early Fiction* (Berkeley: University of California Press, 1965).

It seems plausible that Beckett wanted to find an artistic stance that would free him from the compulsion to travesty the novelistic conventions. How far can one go in the direction of *Murphy*? More demented particulars? More witty persiflage? Even if he could sustain it—*Watt*, in fact, goes as far as one can in that direction—it is possible that the game was not worth the candle to a writer struggling to find his voice in an outmoded form that stifled him. The trilogy supports this conjecture, namely, that in the *Nouvelles* Beckett began experimenting with a literary form that allowed him to exist as author—to come into being, not in compulsive antagonism and mockery, but as a spirit presence, a consciousness somewhere in the background seeking its own identity through the narrative performances, and so finding a new power of immediacy (the Kafkaesque "axe") through the artistic telling of a story.

NOTES TO THE TRILOGY, PRELUDE, CHAPTERS 2–4

1. Samuel Beckett, *Three Novels: Molloy, Malone Dies, The Unnamable* (1955; reprint, New York: Grove, 1958). Subsequent references will be to this text.

2. Samuel Beckett, *How It Is* (New York: Grove, 1964), 38.

3. Quoted in Stephen Spender's introduction to Malcolm Lowry, *Under the Volcano* (New York: New American Library, 1966), xxiii.

4. Samuel Beckett, *Watt* (New York: Grove, 1959), 59.

5. I have borrowed language for these homilies from Pat Conroy's *The Prince of Tides* (1986; reprint, New York: Bantam, 1991).

6. With the exception of his monograph on Proust, Beckett's discursive writings on art have been collected in *Disjecta*. The volume contains his early essay on *Finnegans Wake*, book reviews of 1935–36, his letter to Axel Kaun (the "German Letter" of 1937), and essays on painters that he wrote between 1938 and 1957. "Three Dialogues" is the best known of his aesthetic statements, a seriocomic testing or playing out of his ideas in a parody of a Socratic dialogue.

7. Bert O. States, *The Shape of Paradox:* An Essay on *Waiting for Godot* (Berkeley: University of California Press, 1978), 6.

8. Maurice Blanchot, "Where Now? Who Now?" in *On Beckett: Essays and Criticism*, ed. S. E. Gontarski (New York: Grove, 1986), 144, 147.

9. Andrew K. Kennedy, *Samuel Beckett* (Cambridge: Cambridge University Press, 1989), 141.

10. Anthony Uhlmann, *Beckett and Poststructuralism* (Cambridge: Cambridge University Press, 1999), 184.

11. Uhlmann orbits around the problem of justice, comparing the manner in which it is treated in *The Unnamable*, Levinas's *Totality and Infinity* and Derrida's "Violence and Metaphysics," "Force of Law," and *Spectres de Marx*. The trend in Beckett criticism is to treat *The Unnamable* as a central text for seeing how postmodern theoretical concerns have become the very stuff of fiction.

12. Ibid., 161.

13. Quoted in ibid., 182.

14. Ibid., 184.

15. James Knowlson, *Damned to Fame: The Life of Samuel Beckett* (New York: Simon and Schuster, 1996), 344.

16. Maurice Blanchot, *The Writing of the Disaster*, trans. Ann Smock (Lincoln: University of Nebraska Press, 1986). To my knowledge, Blanchot himself did not connect his writing on *The Unnamable* (1959) with his writing on the Holocaust (1986).

17. He finds strength to hold out in the fairy tale of a master prepared to reward him for heroism by releasing him from torment. "Well done, my child, well done, my son, you may stop, you may go, you are free, you are acquitted, you are pardoned" (*The Unnamable* 310). Pardoned of the necessity for a Second Coming? How fitting the spirit of Beckett if the Unnamable was the rebellious son of God digging in his heels and refusing to be made flesh again. This idea would complete the harmonic progression from Molloy to Malone to the Unnamable.

NOTES TO TORTURE AND ART, PRELUDE, CHAPTERS 5–8

1. Samuel Beckett, *Imagination Dead Imagine*, in *Samuel Beckett: The Complete Short Prose, 1929–1989*, ed. S. E. Gontarski (New York: Grove, 1995), 182. Subsequent references will be to this text.

2. Samuel Beckett in Israel Shenker, "Moody Man of Letters," *The New York Times* (6 May 1956), 2:2; reprinted in James Knowlson and John Pilling, *Frescoes of the Skull: The Later Prose and Drama of Samuel Beckett* (New York: Grove, 1980), 41.

3. Susan D. Brienza, *Samuel Beckett's New Worlds: Style in Metafiction* (Norman: University of Oklahoma Press, 1987), 33–34.

4. Ibid., 33.

5. Elliot Krieger, "Samuel Beckett's *Texts for Nothing*: Explication and Exposition," *Modern Language Notes* 92.5 (December 1977): 993.

6. The three previous quotes are by Rachel Hadas, Edward Hirsch, and John Hollander, speaking of the presence of dream imagery in their poetry, in Roderick Townley, ed., *Night Errands: How Poets Use Dreams* (Pittsburgh: University of Pittsburgh Press, 1998), 45, 58–59, and 70.

7. Samuel Beckett, *Stories* and *Texts for Nothing* (New York: Grove Weidenfeld, 1967). Subsequent references will be to this edition.

8. Franz Kafka, *The Great Wall of China: Stories and Reflections* (1936; reprint, New York: Schocken, 1946), 281.

9. Samuel Beckett, *Endgame: A Play in One Act* (New York: Grove, 1958), 1. Subsequent references will be to this text.

10. Ronald Hayman, *Kafka: A Biography* (New York: Oxford University Press, 1982), 303.

11. Samuel Beckett, *Three Novels by Samuel Beckett: Molloy, Malone Dies, The Unnamable* (1955; reprint, New York: Grove, 1958), 189.

12. Franz Kafka, "A Report to an Academy," *Franz Kafka: The Complete Stories*, ed. Nahum N. Glatzer (1946; reprint, New York: Schocken, 1983), 258.

13. John G. Weightman, "Talking Heads," *Observer Weekend Review* (3 May 1964): 27; Tom Bishop, "Camus and Beckett: Variations on an Absurd Landscape," *Proceedings of the Comparative Literature Symposium* (Texas Tech University, 1975), 8: 53–69; Robert Fothergill, "The Novels of Samuel Beckett. The Search for Identity. The Galley-Slave," *Peace News* (10 December 1965): 5, 10; Alice Hamilton and Kenneth Hamilton, "The Guffaw of the Abderite: Samuel Beckett's Use of Democritus," *Mosaic* 9.2 (winter 1976): 1–14.

14. Neal Oxenhandler, "Seeing and Believing in Dante and Beckett," in *Writing in a Modern Temper: Essays on French Literature and Thought in Honor of Henri Peyre*, ed. Mary Ann Caws (Saratoga, N.Y.: Anma Libri & Co., 1984), 214–23; Philip Terry, "Waiting for God to Go: *How It Is* and *Inferno* VII–VIII," in *Samuel Beckett Today: An Annual Bilingual Review*, vol. 7 (Amsterdam: Editions Rodopi B.V., 1998), 349–60.

15. *Times Literary Supplement* (21 May 1964): 429, reprinted in *Samuel Beckett: The Critical Heritage*, eds. Lawrence Graver and Raymond Federman (Boston: Routledge and Kegan Paul, 1979), 252–54; Dougald McMillan, "Samuel Beckett and the Visual Arts: The Embarrassment of Allegory," in *Samuel Beckett: A Collection of Criticism*, ed. Ruby Cohn (New York: McGraw-Hill, 1975), 121–35.

16. Paul J. Schwartz, "Life and Death in the Mud: A Study of Beckett's *Comment c'est*," *International Fiction Review* 2.1 (January 1975): 43–48.

17. Leo Bersani and Ulysse Dutoit, "Beckett's Sociability," *Raritan: A Quarterly Journal* 12.1 (1992): 1–19.

18. Frederik N. Smith, "Fiction as Composing Process: *How It Is*," in *Samuel Beckett: Humanistic Perspectives*, eds. Morris Beja, S. E. Gontarski, and Pierre Astier (Columbus: Ohio State University Press, 1983), 107–21.

19. Franz Kafka, letter to Oskar Pollak, 27 January 1904, quoted in Ronald Hayman, *Kafka: A Biography* (New York: Oxford University Press, 1982), 41.

20. Quoted in James Knowlson and John Pilling, *Frescoes of the Skull: The Later Prose and Drama of Samuel Beckett* (New York: Grove, 1980), 61. The authors quote these words from *How It Is* in calling the work "Beckett's most intimate and passionate achievement" (61); however, they never give the reader any sense of what makes it so. For example, Knowlson and Pilling: "Beckett's obsession in *How It Is* is very obviously with language" (65). Part two is "Beckett's most sustained attempt to demolish the distinction between subject and object" (69). "[I]t would be wrong to see it as a kind of gloss on Kafka's *In the Penal Colony*, which it superficially resembles" (74). In J. E. Dearlove's *Accommodating the chaos: Samuel Beckett's nonrelational art* (Durham, N.C.: Duke University Press, 1982), the novel is "an acceptance, if not celebration, of the life of the imagination" (85). In the ambivalent world of the novel, "where everything is self-consciously fictive," nothing is certain; "correction and revision can be flatly announced" (105). What then? "[T]he work explores the fluid universe of the mind and its imagination" (106).

In H. Porter Abbott's "Beginning again: The post-narrative art of *Texts for nothing* and *How it is*," in *The Cambridge Companion to Beckett*, ed. John Pilling (New York: Cambridge University Press, 1994), the novel is about travestying epic narrative, its raison d'être, "to stupefy" (115). Beckett, "our discreator" (116), creates a poetry in which "sound . . . arrogat[es] to itself the place traditionally held by meaning" (120). It's hard to find an "axe" in these discussions.

21. Patrick J. Moore, "Ars Poetica: A Study of Samuel Beckett's *How It Is* (*Comment C'est*)," *Journal of Evolutionary Psychology* 17.1–2 (1996): 85.

22. Samuel Beckett, *Disjecta: Miscellaneous Writings and a Dramatic Fragment*, ed. Ruby Cohn (London: John Calder, 1983). See especially "Three Dialogues" and "German Letter" of 1937.

23. Bert O. States, *The Shape of Paradox: An Essay on* Waiting for Godot (Berkeley: University of California Press 1978), 6.

24. Miklós Radnóti, "Fragment," in *The Complete Poetry*, ed. and trans. Emery George (Ann Arbor, Mich.: Ardis, 1980), 267.

25. William Carlos Williams, quoted by Roderick Townley, ed., as epigraph to *Night Errands: How Poets Use Dreams* (Pittsburgh: University of Pittsburgh Press, 1998).

26. James Knowlson and John Pilling, *Frescoes of the Skull: The Later Prose and Drama of Samuel Beckett* (New York: Grove, 1980), 167.

27. Ibid., 158.

28. Ibid., 160.

29. Ibid., 165.

30. Ibid., 158.

31. Ibid., 162.

32. Ruby Cohn, *A Beckett Canon* (Ann Arbor: University of Michigan Press, 2001), 312, 313.

33. Franz Kafka, "In the Penal Colony," in *Franz Kafka: The Complete Stories*, ed. Nahum N. Glatzer (1946; reprint, New York: Schocken, 1983), 140. Subsequent references will be to this text.

34. Samuel Beckett, *The Lost Ones*, in *Samuel Beckett: The Complete Short Prose, 1929–1989*, ed. S. E. Gontarski (New York: Grove, 1995), 202. Subsequent references will be to this text.

35. *Purgatorio, The Divine Comedy*, Canto IV, line 122, ed. Paolo Milano, trans. Laurence Binyon (1947; reprint, New York: Viking, 1955), 207.

NOTES TO CHAPTER 9

1. See Gabriele Schwab, "The Politics of Small Differences: Beckett's *The Unnamable*," in *Engagement and Indifference: Beckett and the Political*, eds. Henry Sussman and Christopher Devenney (Albany: State University of New York Press, 2001), 42–57. Schwab analyzes the novel as a grotesque language game.

2. For example, Ruby Cohn, whom I will discuss in the text. Ruby Cohn, "*Watt* in the Light of *The Castle*," *Comparative Literature* 13 (1961). Edith Kern argues that because truth is inaccessible in *Watt* and *The Castle*, an omniscient narrator is impossible. Hence, the first-person consciousness that guides us through the text on a search for truth becomes a stand-in for the author, creating what she calls an "author-hero" in texts that are themselves expressions of the artistic mission (110). Edith Kern, "Reflections on the Castle and Mr. Knott's House: Kafka and Beckett," *Proceedings of the Comparative Literature Symposium: Franz Kafka: His Place in World Literature, 28–29 January 1971*, ed. Wolodymyr T. Zyla (Lubbock: The Texas Tech Press, 1971). Charles Bernheimer has argued that in *Watt* and *The Castle* the need of K. and Watt to "read" themselves or their own desires is undermined by the writerly impulse toward displacement and fragmentation; he says that "Beckett inherited from Kafka the literary structure of the aporetic quest, the quest for readerly knowledge that becomes inextricably implicated in the

process of writerly displacement" (23). Charles Bernheimer, "*Watt*'s in *The Castle*: The Aporetic Quest in Kafka and Beckett," *Newsletter of the Kafka Society of America* 6.1–2 (1982): 19–24.

3. Cohn, "*Watt* in the Light of *The Castle*," 158.

4. Franz Kafka, *The Great Wall of China: Stories and Reflections* (1936; reprint, New York: Schocken, 1946), 267. Subsequent references will be to this text.

5. Samuel Beckett, *Watt* (New York: Grove, 1959), 76. Subsequent references will be to this text.

6. Cohn, "*Watt* in the Light of *The Castle*,"155.

7. Ibid., 158.

8. Hans H. Hiebel, "Beckett's Television Plays and Kafka's Late Stories," *Samuel Beckett Today/Aujourd'hui: An Annual Bilingual Review* 6, ed. Marius Buning, Matthijs Engelberts, and Sjef Houppermans (Atlanta, Ga.: Rodopi, 1997), 325.

9. For example, George H. Szanto has argued that these authors (along with Robbe-Grillet) show "that the writer's province is no longer the impossible environment, but is instead the only knowledge any one man can have, the knowledge he attains through his perceptions" (7–8). Hence, these authors use an immediate and sustained point of view, which reflects their "[concern] with process rather than with established fact" (9); the reader himself, "without the intercession of critical insight" (13) essentially "'becomes' the protagonist," forced to "engage in the analytic process" (12). George H. Szanto, *Narrative Consciousness: Structure and Perception in the Fiction of Kafka, Beckett, and Robbe-Grillet* (Austin: University of Texas Press, 1972).

According to Daniel Albright, Beckett and Kafka are both sustained and frustrated by the power of the imagination. For while they are among the most imaginative writers, in their fiction imagination constantly conjures up false images that distract from the search for the truth. By constantly dispelling these false images, Albright argues, Beckett and Kafka effectively hint at a truth: "If the thud, the shock of palpable reality cannot be manufactured, it can be alluded to, witnessed by its absence" (10). Daniel Albright, *Representation and the Imagination: Beckett, Kafka, Nabokov, and Schoenberg* (Chicago: University of Chicago Press, 1981).

Jina Politi has argued that in Kafka's short story "The Judgment," as in Peter's denial of Christ in the Bible, the subject must recognize the inability of self-definition, must invariably recognize himself as object; in Beckett's *Not I*, however, Mouth persistently defies this trend, demanding the right to author her own fictions, hence "the power of a discourse which is stronger than consciousness . . . is here utterly frustrated" (353). Jina Politi, "Not (Not I)," *Journal of Literature & Theology* 6.4 (December 1992): 345–55.

Geoff Wade's Marxist reading has argued that " '[r]edemption' *is* held out" even in the seeming pessimism and gloom in the works of Beckett and Kafka, since "to ensure the ultimate coming to pass of that redemption we must ceaselessly spell out just what we are being redeemed from (or averting, as the case may be)" (128). Geoff Wade, "Marxism and modernist aesthetics: reading Kafka and Beckett," in *The politics of pleasure: Aesthetics and cultural theory*, ed. Stephen Regan (Philadelphia: Open University Press, 1992), 109–32.

E. V. Călin has compared the use of silences, or gaps, in Kafka and Beckett, suggesting that in Kafka, the gaps "appear to recall—on a stylistic plane —an *a prioric* silence: silence as an incomprehensible universe's answer to the queries of human conscience" (260). In Beckett's work, Călin says, silence always bubbles to the surface, as the characters—who simultaneously dread and desire the impending final silence—babble through the texts, attempting to delay that end: "[t]he steadily restored end gives rise, in Beckett's novels, to the discourse that records the extinction, the discourse that, while striving for final silence, has to record the death of discourse" (261). E. V. Călin, "From Ellipsis into Silence in Contemporary Literature," in *Expression, Communication and Experience in Literature and Language: Proceedings of the XII Congress of the International Federation for Modern Languages and Literatures, 20–26 August 1972*, ed. Ronald G. Popperwell (Leeds: The Modern Humanities Research Association, 1973), 259–62.

10. Kafka, *Great Wall*, 267–68.

11. Franz Kafka, *The Castle* (1926; reprint, New York: Schocken, 1974), 335–36. Subsequent references will be to this text.

12. Samuel Beckett, *The Unnamable*, in *Three Novels by Samuel Beckett: Molloy, Malone Dies, The Unnamable* (1955; reprint, New York: Grove, 1958), 338. Subsequent references will be to this text.

13. Israel Shenker, "Moody Man of Letters: A Portrait of Samuel Beckett, Author of the Puzzling 'Waiting for Godot,'" *The New York Times* (6 May 1956), 2:2.

14. Franz Kafka, *The Diaries of Franz Kafka 1910–1913*, ed. Max Brod, trans. Joseph Kresh (1948; reprint, New York, Schocken, 1968), 317. Subsequent references will be to this text.

15. Franz Kafka, *The Trial*, trans. Willa and Edwin Muir (1937; reprint, New York: Random House, 1956), 167. Subsequent references will be to this text.

16. See Thomas Mann, "Homage" in Franz Kafka, *The Castle*, ix–xvii.

17. Franz Kafka, *Letters to Friends, Family, and Editors*, trans. Richard Winston and Clara Winston (1958; reprint, New York: Schocken, 1977), 102. Subsequent references will be to this text.

18. Quoted in Peter Mailloux, *A Hesitation before Birth: The Life of Franz Kafka* (London: Associated University Presses, 1989), 359.

19. Ernst Pawel, *The Nightmare of Reason: A Life of Franz Kafka* (New York: Farrar, Straus & Giroux, 1984), 216.

20. Franz Kafka, *Letters to Felice*, eds. Erich Heller and Jürgen Born, trans. James Stern and Elisabeth Duckworth (1967; reprint, New York: Schocken, 1973), 524–25.

21. Pawel, *The Nightmare of Reason*, 279.

22. Letter from Milena Jesenská to Max Brod, in Max Brod, *Franz Kafka: A Biography* (1937; reprint, New York: Schocken, 1963), 230.

23. Ibid., 234.

24. Mailloux, *A Hesitation before Birth,* 478–80.

25. Franz Kafka, *The Diaries of Franz Kafka 1914–1923*, ed. Max Brod, trans. Martin Greenberg (1949; reprint, New York: Schocken, 1968), 197.

26. Beckett, *The Expelled*, in *Samuel Beckett: The Complete Short Prose, 1929–1989*, ed. S. E. Gontarski (New York: Grove, 1995), 48.

27. Beckett, *The Calmative*, in *The Complete Short Prose,* 61.

28. Ibid., 62.

29. Beckett, *Stories* and *Texts for Nothing*, 119.

30. Ibid., 125.

31. Ibid., 127.

Bibliography

Abbott, H. Porter. "Beginning again: the post-narrative art of *Texts for Nothing* and *How It Is*." In *The Cambridge Companion to Beckett*. Edited by John Pilling. Cambridge: Cambridge University Press, 1994. 106–23.

Acheson, James. *Samuel Beckett's Artistic Theory and Practice: Criticism, Drama and Early Fiction*. New York: St. Martin's Press, 1997.

Albright, Daniel. *Representation and the Imagination: Beckett, Kafka, Nabokov, and Schoenberg*. Chicago: University of Chicago Press, 1981.

Amis, Martin. *Experience*. New York: Hyperion, 2000.

Andonian, Cathleen Culotta. *Samuel Beckett: a reference guide*. Boston: G. K. Hall, 1989.

Barale, Michèle Aina, and Rubin Rabinovitz. *A Kwic Concordance to Samuel Beckett's Trilogy:* Molloy, Malone Dies, *and* The Unnamable. 2 vols. New York: Garland, 1988.

Beckett, Samuel. *Disjecta: Miscellaneous Writings and a Dramatic Fragment*. Edited by Ruby Cohn. London: John Calder, 1983.

——. *Endgame: A Play in One Act*. New York: Grove Press, 1958.

——. *How It Is*. Translated by the author. New York: Grove Press, 1964.

——. *Samuel Beckett: The Complete Short Prose, 1929–1989*. Edited by S. E. Gontarski. New York: Grove Press, 1995.

——. *Stories* and *Texts for Nothing*. New York: Grove Weidenfeld, 1967.

——. *Three Novels by Samuel Beckett: Molloy, Malone Dies, The Unnamable*. 1955. Reprint, New York: Grove Press, 1958.

——. *Waiting for Godot*. New York: Grove Press, 1954.

——. *Watt*. New York: Grove Press, 1959.

Begam, Richard. *Samuel Beckett and the End of Modernity*. Stanford, Calif.: Stanford University Press, 1996.

Bernheimer, Charles. "*Watt*'s in *The Castle*: The Aporetic Quest in Kafka and Beckett." *Newsletter of the Kafka Society of America* 6.1–2 (1982): 19–24.

Bernstein, Jay. "Philosophy's Refuge: Adorno in Beckett." In *Philosophers' Poets*. Edited by David Wood. New York: Routledge, 1990. 177–91.

Bersani, Leo, and Ulysse Dutoit. *Arts of Impoverishment: Beckett, Rothko, Resnais*. Cambridge: Harvard University Press, 1993.

_____. "Beckett's Sociability." *Raritan: A Quarterly Journal* 12.1 (1992): 1–19.

Bishop, Tom. "Camus and Beckett: Variations on an Absurd Landscape." *Proceedings of the Comparative Literature Symposium*. Texas Tech University 8 (1975): 53–69.

Blanchot, Maurice. "Where Now? Who Now?" In *On Beckett: Essays and Criticism*. Edited by S. E. Gontarski. New York: Grove Press, 1986. 141–49.

_____. *The Writing of the Disaster*. Translated by Ann Smock. Lincoln: University of Nebraska Press, 1986.

Bloom, Harold, ed. *Samuel Beckett's Endgame*. New York: Chelsea House Press, 1998.

Brater, Enoch. *The Drama in the Text: Beckett's Late Fiction*. New York: Oxford University Press, 1994.

Brienza, Susan D. *Samuel Beckett's New Worlds: Style in Metafiction*. Norman: University of Oklahoma Press, 1987.

Brod, Max. *Franz Kafka: A Biography*. 1937. Reprint, New York: Schocken Books, 1963.

Călin, E. V. "From Ellipsis into Silence in Contemporary Literature." *Expression, Communication and Experience in Literature and Language: Proceedings of the XII Congress of the International Federation for Modern Languages and Literatures, 20–26 August 1972*. Edited by Ronald G. Popperwell. Leeds: The Modern Humanities Research Association, 1973. 259–62.

Cohn, Ruby. *Back to Beckett*. Princeton: Princeton University Press, 1973.

_____. *A Beckett Canon*. Ann Arbor: University of Michigan Press, 2001.

_____. "*Watt* in the Light of *The Castle*." *Comparative Literature* 13 (1961): 154–66.

Conroy, Pat. *The Prince of Tides*. 1986. Reprint, New York: Bantam, 1991.

Cousineau, Thomas J. *After the Final No: Samuel Beckett's Trilogy*. Newark: University of Delaware Press, 1999.

Dante Alighieri. *The Divine Comedy, Inferno*. Edited and translated by Robert M. Durling. New York: Oxford University Press, 1997.

_____. *The Divine Comedy, Purgatorio*. Edited by Paolo Milano. Translated by Laurence Binyon. 1947. Reprint, New York: Viking Press, 1955.

Dearlove, J. E. *Accommodating the chaos: Samuel Beckett's nonrelational art*. Durham, N.C.: Duke University Press, 1982.

Federman, Raymond. "Beckett [f]or Nothing." In *Comparative Literary Dimensions: Essays in Honor of Melvin J. Friedman*. Edited by Jay L. Halio and Ben Siegel. Newark: University of Delaware Press, 2000. 97–108.

_____. *Journey to Chaos: Samuel Beckett's Early Fiction*. Berkeley: University of California Press, 1965.

Federman, Raymond, and John Fletcher. *Samuel Beckett: His Works and His Critics; an Essay in Bibliography*. Berkeley: University of California Press, 1970.

Finney, Brian. "*Assumption* to *Lessness*: Beckett's shorter fiction." In *Beckett the shape changer*. Edited by Katharine Worth. London: Routledge and Kegan Paul, 1975. 63–83.

Fothergill, Robert. "The Novels of Samuel Beckett. The Search for Identity. The Galley-Slave." *Peace News* (10 December 1965): 5, 10.

Graver, Lawrence, and Raymond Federman, eds. *Samuel Beckett: The Critical Heritage.* Boston: Routledge and Kegan Paul, 1979.

Hamilton, Alice, and Kenneth Hamilton. "The Guffaw of the Abderite: Samuel Beckett's Use of Democritus." *Mosaic* 9.2 (winter 1976): 1–14.

Hayman, Ronald. *Kafka: A Biography.* New York: Oxford University Press, 1982.

Henning, Sylvie Debevec. *Beckett's Critical Complicity: Carnival, Contestation, and Tradition.* Lexington: University of Kentucky Press, 1988.

Hiebel, Hans H. "Beckett's Television Plays and Kafka's Late Stories." *Samuel Beckett Today/Aujourd'hui: An Annual Bilingual Review* 6. Edited by Marius Buning, Matthijs Engelberts, and Sjef Houppermans. Atlanta, Ga.: Rodopi, 1997. 313–27.

Kafka, Franz. *The Castle.* 1926. Reprint, New York: Schocken Books, 1974.

————. *The Complete Stories.* Edited by Nahum N. Glatzer. 1946. Reprint, New York: Schocken Books, 1983.

————. *The Diaries of Franz Kafka 1910–1913.* Edited by Max Brod. Translated by Joseph Kresh. 1948. Reprint, New York: Schocken Books, 1968.

————. *The Diaries of Franz Kafka 1914–1923.* Edited by Max Brod. Translated by Martin Greenberg. 1949. Reprint, New York: Schocken Books, 1968.

————. *The Great Wall of China: Stories and Reflections.* 1936. Reprint, New York: Schocken Books, 1946.

————. *Letters to Felice.* Edited by Erich Heller and Jürgen Born. Translated by James Stern and Elisabeth Duckworth. 1967. Reprint, New York: Schocken Books, 1973.

————. *Letters to Friends, Family, and Editors.* Translated by Richard and Clara Winston. 1958. Reprint, New York: Schocken Books, 1977.

————. *The Trial.* Translated by Willa and Edwin Muir. 1937. Reprint, New York: Random House, 1956.

Katz, Daniel. *Saying I No More: Subjectivity and Consciousness in the Prose of Samuel Beckett.* Evanston, Ill.: Northwestern University Press, 1999.

Kennedy, Andrew K. *Samuel Beckett.* Cambridge: Cambridge University Press, 1989.

Kern, Edith. "Reflections on the Castle and Mr. Knott's House: Kafka and Beckett." *Proceedings of the Comparative Literature Symposium, Franz Kafka: His Place in World Literature, 28–29 January 1971.* Edited by Wolodymyr T. Zyla. Lubbock: The Texas Tech Press, 1971. 97–111.

Knowlson, James. *Damned to Fame: The Life of Samuel Beckett.* New York: Simon and Schuster, 1996.

Knowlson, James, and John Pilling. *Frescoes of the Skull: The Later Prose and Drama of Samuel Beckett.* New York: Grove Press, 1980.

Krieger, Elliot. "Samuel Beckett's *Texts for Nothing*: Explication and Exposition." *Modern Language Notes* 92.5 (December 1977): 987–1000.

Mailloux, Peter. *A Hesitation before Birth: The Life of Franz Kafka.* London: Associated University Presses, 1989.

Mann, Thomas. "Homage." In *The Castle*. By Franz Kafka. 1926. Reprint, New York: Schocken Books, 1974. ix–xvii.

McMillan, Dougald. "Samuel Beckett and the Visual Arts: The Embarrassment of Allegory." In *Samuel Beckett: A Collection of Criticism*. Edited by Ruby Cohn. New York: McGraw-Hill, 1975. 121–35.

Moore, Patrick J. "Ars Poetica: A Study of Samuel Beckett's *How It Is (Comment c'est)*." *Journal of Evolutionary Psychology* 17.1–2 (1996): 82–89.

Murphy, P. J. *Reconstructing Beckett: Language for Being in Samuel Beckett's Fiction*. Toronto: University of Toronto Press, 1990.

Murphy, P. J., Werner Huber, Rolf Breuer, and Konrad Schoell. *Critique of Beckett Criticism: A Guide to Research in English, French, and German*. Columbia, S.C.: Camden House, 1994.

O'Hara, J. D. *Samuel Beckett's Hidden Drives: Structural Uses of Depth Psychology*. Gainesville: University Press of Florida, 1997.

Oxenhandler, Neal. "Seeing and Believing in Dante and Beckett." In *Writing in a Modern Temper. Essays on French Literature and Thought in Honor of Henri Peyre*. Edited by Mary Ann Caws. Saratoga, N.Y.: Anma Libri & Co., 1984. 214–23.

Pawel, Ernst. *The Nightmare of Reason: A Life of Franz Kafka*. New York: Farrar, Straus & Giroux, 1984.

Politi, Jina. "Not (Not I)." *Journal of Literature & Theology* 6.4 (December 1992): 345–55.

Radnóti, Miklós. "Fragment." In *The Complete Poetry*. Edited and translated by Emery George. Ann Arbor, Mich.: Ardis, 1980. 267.

Rose, Marilyn Gaddis. "The Lyrical Structure of Beckett's *Texts for Nothing*." *Novel: A Forum on Fiction* 4.3 (spring 1971): 223–30.

Schwab, Gabriele. "The Politics of Small Differences: Beckett's *The Unnamable*." In *Engagement and Indifference: Beckett and the Political*. Edited by Henry Sussman and Christopher Devenney. Albany: State University of New York Press, 2001. 42–57.

Schwartz, Paul J. "Life and Death in the Mud: A Study of Beckett's *Comment c'est*." *International Fiction Review* 2.1 (January 1975): 43–48.

Shenker, Israel. "Moody Man of Letters: A Portrait of Samuel Beckett, Author of the Puzzling 'Waiting for Godot.'" *The New York Times* (6 May 1956), 2: 2–3.

Smith, Frederik N. "Fiction as Composing Process: *How It Is*." In *Samuel Beckett: Humanistic Perspectives*. Edited by Morris Beja, S. E. Gontarski, and Pierre Astier. Columbus: Ohio State University Press, 1983. 107–21.

Spender, Stephen. Introduction to Malcolm Lowry, *Under the Volcano*. New York: New American Library, 1966. vii–xxvi.

States, Bert O. *The Shape of Paradox: An Essay on Waiting for Godot*. Berkeley: University of California Press, 1978.

Szanto, George H. *Narrative Consciousness: Structure and Perception in the Fiction of Kafka, Beckett, and Robbe-Grillet*. Austin: University of Texas Press, 1972.

Terry, Philip. "Waiting for God to Go: *How It Is* and *Inferno* VII–VIII." *Samuel Beckett Today: An Annual Bilingual Review*. Vol. 7. Amsterdam: Editions Rodopi B. V., 1998. 349–60.

Thiher, Allen. "Wittgenstein, Heidegger, the Unnamable, and Some Thoughts on the Status of Voice in Fiction." In *Samuel Beckett: Humanistic Perspectives*. Edited by Morris Beja, S. E. Gontarski, and Pierre Astier. Columbus: Ohio State University Press, 1983.

Townley, Roderick, ed. *Night Errands: How Poets Use Dreams*. Pittsburgh: University of Pittsburgh Press, 1998.

Uhlmann, Anthony. *Beckett and Poststructuralism*. Cambridge: Cambridge University Press, 1999.

Wade, Geoff. "Marxism and modernist aesthetics: reading Kafka and Beckett." In *The politics of pleasure: Aesthetics and cultural theory*. Edited by Stephen Regan. Philadelphia: Open University Press, 1992. 109–32.

Webb, Eugene. *Samuel Beckett: A Study of His Novels*. London: Peter Owen, 1972.

Weightman, John. "Talking Heads." *Observer Weekend Review* (3 May 1964): 27.

West, Paul. "Deciphering a Beckett Fiction on His Birthday." *Parnassus: Poetry in Review* 11.2 (fall/winter 1983 and spring/summer 1984): 319–22.

Worton, Michael. "*Waiting for Godot* and *Endgame*: theatre as text." In *The Cambridge Companion to Beckett*. Edited by John Pilling. Cambridge: Cambridge University Press, 1994. 67–87.

Wright, Iain. "'What Matter Who's Speaking?' Beckett, the Authorial Subject and Contemporary Critical Theory." *The Southern Review* 16.1 (March 1983): 5–30.

Index

185